I thoroughly enjoyed *He Cal...* woven throughout the book pull... transforming power and enable y... ...eautiful journey for yourself. I recommend *He Calls Me Beloved* and know it will truly be a gift to its readers.

Joy Kirkpatrick
Psychotherapist

Pamela Marhad's book, *He Calls Me Beloved*, is an inspiring story about learning to hear God's voice and how he transformed her life and brought emotional healing. Pam is a talented writer, and many will be blessed by reading her testimony.

C. Stevens Schell
Senior Pastor
Northwest Church, Federal Way, WA

Pamela Marhad has taken a great and lovely risk by letting us in on her, and our, humanity. Veering between Psalm-like writings and straightforward journal entries, she allows us, and invites us, to face the difficulties of finitude and the struggle and joys of embracing God's accepting presence. Her questions for reflection and discussion at the end of the book are helpful for those who, moved by her story, will ask, "So where do I go from here?" This is a very helpful book.

Gary R. Sattler
Dr. Theology, Psych. D.
Fuller Theological Seminary, Adj. Prof.

HE CALLS ME
Beloved

HE CALLS ME
Beloved

RESPONDING *to the* CALL *to* INTIMACY

PAMELA MARHAD

Pleasant Word (a division of WinePress Publishing, PO Box 428, Enumclaw, WA 98022) functions only as book publisher. As such, the ultimate design, content, editorial accuracy, and views expressed or implied in this work are those of the author.

Unless otherwise noted, all Scriptures are taken from the *Holy Bible, New International Version®, NIV®*. Copyright © 1973, 1978, 1984 by the International Bible Society. Used by permission of Zondervan. All rights reserved.

Verses marked AMPLIFIED are taken from *The Amplified Bible, Old Testament* copyright ©1965, 1987 by the Zondervan Corporation. The Amplified New Testament copyright ©1958, 1987 by The Lockman Foundation. Used by permission.

Verses marked MSG are taken from *The Message*. Copyright © by Eugene H. Peterson 1993, 1994, 1995, 1996, 2000, 2001, 2002. Used by permission of NavPress Publishing Group.

ISBN 13: 978-1-4141-1314-2
ISBN 10: 1-4141-1314-5
Library of Congress Catalog Card Number: 2008910537

To George—my husband, soul mate,
and dearest friend

Contents

CHAPTER 1

The Invitation

——❦❦❦——

THE INVITATION CAME, *written by his own hand and addressed to me.*

I held it, laughing at myself. Surely not! There's been some mistake. I shouldn't even consider it. I can just hear the voices: "What presumption! Imagine her daring to attend this event!"—and then the shame of being sent away.

But then again, perhaps if I stay in the shadows, I won't be discovered and made to leave.

It would be enough, and worth the risk of discovery, just to be with the beautiful ones, to hear their joy and see their love. Perhaps I would even have a quick glimpse of him—it would be enough.

Full of misgivings, I decided to go.

I dressed in white, as the invitation had requested, and made my way to the Great Hall.

The large doors stood open, and golden light poured out into the darkness of the night. I searched, but finding no other entrance, I stepped cautiously into the room, looking for a shadowed place to hide. Imagine my panic when, finding no shadows, I stood exposed in that golden light.

I kept my head down, waiting for the voices: "Imposter! Uninvited guest! Cast her out!" I waited…

When I dared at last to lift my eyes and face my accusers, I saw him across the room. Every face but his was hidden by the light. He was smiling in my direction, so I quickly stepped aside to make room for the object of his welcome. But glancing behind me, I saw only the open door and the darkness.

Confused and embarrassed, I looked once more at him, waiting for the recognition, the disappointment, to appear on his face. But his smile held me—me!

"There's been a mistake," I stammered. Yet he walked toward me. I could see myself reflected in his eyes. I looked at him, searching his face. So afraid to believe what I saw there.

Then he stood before me, holding out his hand. "At last you have come, beloved."

This love story began many years ago with an invitation from Jesus to a young woman who had come to the conclusion that she was unlovable. It is a story of patient, passionate pursuit of His beloved by Love Himself.

This is my story, because mine is the only story I can truly tell. But my hope is that where our stories are similar, you will be drawn in a fresh way to the One who invites you to come a little closer and hear Him call you His "beloved."

My love story with Jesus is written in the form of conversations I have had with Him as He has taught me what it means to be His beloved. I have had to learn, as well as unlearn, many things along the way. Much of what He has spoken to me I still struggle to receive and live out in my life. Sometimes I get discouraged, seeing how little progress I have made in understanding what it means to be God's beloved. But then I am reminded that in the light of eternity, the adventure of transformation has just begun!

When I started writing down my conversations with God, I had no intention of others ever seeing them. I knew the exception might be family members, who would one distant day come across them as they sorted through the accumulated stuff of my lifetime. But that would be when I was no longer around to care what they might think of me.

Had I known that God would one day ask me to expose the ups and downs of my soul's clumsy journey, I'm sure I would have practiced more silent, rather than written, prayer. But one morning I heard the Lord say to me, "You have been taking good notes for quite a long while. Now it's time to put them in an useable form."

So began the process of sorting through and putting in order portions of what I had written down from my conversations with God. As I worked on this project, the idea was planted and began to grow that God had led me to write down His words of comfort and counsel because they weren't meant for me alone. There were others who would also be encouraged by them.

Perhaps you are one of those. If so, I hope you will step right into this story and hear God call *you* His beloved. For your story and my story are best lived out in the context of His extraordinary love for us. Knowing we are God's beloved gives us a solid and true beginning for our stories, steadies and guides us through each page and chapter that follows, and then guarantees us the very happiest of ever afters.

ENTER IN …

I have loved you with an everlasting love; I have drawn you with loving-kindness.

—Jeremiah 31:3

Pause a moment and read this verse to yourself, inserting your name after the word "you." It suddenly becomes personal and immediate, doesn't it? In this moment, the King of Love is drawing you to Himself.

CHAPTER 2

Love Song

SHE FELT MOST comfortable sitting near the door of the Great Room. That she found herself in this beautiful place at all was the stuff of fairytales. And, like Cinderella, she knew she would need to make a quick escape when the spell was broken.

But for now, reality could wait. For these few, lovely moments she would sit in the glorious light and beauty that surrounded her and pretend she belonged in this joyful crowd.

It was faint at first—just the hint of a Song stirring in the air around her. She caught a few familiar words and unconsciously began humming and lightly tapping her foot. Slowly, imperceptibly, the Song drew closer and danced on the edges of her awareness. She began to feel the stirring of the air around her—warm, inviting. She swayed slightly to the Song in the warm breeze flowing over her.

Irresistibly drawn by the Song, she rose to her feet. With hesitant steps, she began to follow as it led her away from her place by the door. Awkward at first, she grew more graceful, keeping in step with the Song as it led her deeper into the Great Room. Her lips began to give voice to the unfamiliar joy breaking free within her.

The Song entered her soul and became her Song. New chords, new words she'd not sung before, carried her deeper and deeper into the room and farther and farther from the open door.

The Song within her descended into valleys of wailing discord and then rose on currents of beauty and harmony. Raw, powerful, it dipped and rose on chords of truth, on words of longing, exposing every hidden, lifeless thing and flooding her with light.

Dancing, singing, the Song led her back across the room to stand before the open door. All became still as she considered the scene before her. The door framed all that was familiar. The twilight gray of the evening sky wooed her with a promise of shelter from the penetrating light of the room. She had often hidden in the twilight; it gave a grim sort of comfort. A well-worn path beckoned a return to independent, solitary ways—so unlike the crowded, light-filled room behind her.

She paused only a moment. The Song rose within her as she stepped forward and closed the door, shutting out the twilight. She turned toward the light. She would sing a new Song—a Song set free—her heart's Song.

"Jesus loves me, this I know, for the Bible tells me so" are the words to a wonderful little song most of us are familiar with. Simple and foundational, it's a good place to start in our understanding of God's love for us. The Bible says it—so it's true.

But I found it very difficult to move from this simple statement of fact to the actual heart knowledge and experience of God's love for me. Trust was slow to develop in my relationship with God. In fact, for many years I kept the back door of our relationship open. At the first sign of betrayal, I wanted out.

Though I take full responsibility for my own sinful choices and rebellious heart, I believe our family of origin has much to do with the way we view God and how we relate to Him. God has given human parents the monumental task of representing Him to their children. And if our parents don't know Him, the view can be very distorted.

My own father, though a person of humor and charm, was ruled by strong prejudices passed on to him by his father. He would voice his dogmatic and prejudiced opinions in frequent tirades that allowed for no disagreement or discussion. To express a differing opinion would set off one of these tirades and invite ridicule and rejection. So keeping one's thoughts to oneself was the way to maintain peace in our family, and I became very good at it. The unspoken rule of our home was: *keep daddy happy.* But each member of our family paid a high price for letting the spirit of fear and prejudice have such a powerful place in our home.

As the years passed, I came to many wrong conclusions about myself and other people. These conclusions had—and to some extent continue to have—influence on how I relate to God and others.

When, as a young woman of 20, I gave my heart to Jesus, my main concern was to win His approval and keep Him happy with me. The idea that God loved me just as I was and wanted a lasting friendship with me was very difficult to believe. I understood His desire for me to serve Him, but loving relationship was something altogether different—even frightening.

Of course, it is impossible to settle in and grow a relationship when one party is in constant fright and flight mode, as I was. Consequently, my walk with God was a roller-coaster ride of highs and lows. When all was going well, I felt loved and close to Him. When life frightened or unsettled me, quite often I experienced what felt like an emotional free fall into a dark pit.

Where would any of us be if God in His loving-kindness didn't pursue us right into the pit and rescue us? But He does, and He did, and slowly, slowly, I learned that His love for me was a secure refuge where I could finally shut the door and be "at home."

Gently, almost imperceptibly, He had moved me from the sidelines of my fear and distrust right out onto the dance floor with Him, where He began to teach me to move in step with His Spirit and sing the Song He had placed in my heart.

Learning to Float

As I mentioned, learning to trust God's love for me has taken a long time. I have found it especially hard to rest in His love when I'm disappointed in myself and feel He must be disappointed as well. I grew up equating disappointment or disapproval with rejection, and rejection was my greatest fear.

One day He used a picture to show me how I struggled in this area. I saw a person flailing around in the ocean. There was terror on her face. Her arms moved wildly in an effort to stay afloat. Here's what the Lord said:

Beloved, this is a picture of your inability to rest in the ocean of My love that surrounds you. My love will support you, but to learn this, you must practice trust. Just as learning to float in the ocean requires trusting the water to hold you up, resting in My love requires that you trust Me.

Trust Me to love and accept you even when you feel like a failure. Trust that your life isn't a mistake. Trust Me to teach and instruct you in the way I have chosen for you. Trust Me to keep you from missing My will. Trust that even though you can't see the future, I have plans and purposes for your life. Trust Me, beloved, and let your heart rest in My love.

The Pleasure of Your Company

The words from Psalm 37:4 came to mind one day, as if the Lord was speaking them directly to me: *"Delight yourself in Me and I will give you the desires of your heart."* Then I heard:

Beloved, whenever you take the time to sit with Me, I will meet with you.

Lord, several thoughts come to mind on hearing this—one I'm not proud of. I sense first of all Your incredible humility. To meet with me when *I* take the time. Again, You are teaching me about the nature of Your love: unconditional, always giving, approachable, patient—irresistible!

Unfortunately, I also had the thought that You sound like a pushover.

Did I really just hear You laugh and say, *"Yes, I'm a pushover for your love, daughter"*?

I'll meet you more than half way, beloved. In fact, I am always eager for your company. I never tire of you. To share life with you is a delight. We've just begun to live life together, and the joy that awaits us is beyond your wildest imaginings. Walk with Me quietly, patiently, into the adventure of a lifetime! *"No eye has seen, no ear has heard, no mind has conceived what God has prepared for those who love him…" (1 Corinthians 2:9).*

A Good Father

Lord, You have blessed us, but I have the feeling that I'm getting away with something I don't deserve and that it's just a matter of time until You take away the good things and bring loss and suffering. I know that even as I try to describe what I feel deep inside, there is a heart and attitude change needed. Why can't I just receive Your blessings and trust You without fearing loss?

Because you are holding on too tightly to the good things, as if you fear I will snatch them away if you are not vigilant to protect them. And, yes, it is a trust issue.

You're not "getting away" with something, daughter. Every good and perfect gift comes from Me. It pleased Me to give you your family, your home, and all that you love. I provide for My own—I am a good Father. Does a good father begrudge his child the things that bring that child joy? Does a good father wait and plan for the time he will snatch away his child's dearest treasures? Of course not.

But a good father may ask his child to relinquish something she treasures. Do you see the difference? That is where trust comes in. A good father shows his child in many ways how strong and unchanging his love is. The child learns by experience that she can trust her father to do his best for her, even when her father must make decisions the child cannot understand.

Beloved, it is My desire to care and provide for you all your days. You can relax in My generous, unfailing love for you. You may not always understand what I am doing, but you can be sure that no detail of your need will ever escape My notice.

I want you to rest now and give up your vigilance of self-protection.

Love to Stretch Out In

Lord, I know that You want me to be free of the fear of failure. I also know that fear has held me back at times from venturing out with You into new things. But I choose now to trust You; I choose to live freely and creatively as You lead the way.

My heart is your home, daughter, and it is big and roomy enough to allow for all the creativity and freedom for which I designed you. There is nothing confining or restricting in My love. Dare to stretch out in My love. Failure will only come from not trying.

Persevering Love

Thank You, Lord, for Your love that perseveres even when I give You a hard time.

Daughter, loving you isn't hard for Me.

Lord, is this truly Your voice I'm hearing?

Beloved, you have difficulty believing My words of love for you because you think you are unlovable.

Then, Lord, please give me a greater capacity to receive Your love and give You my love.

Yes, that is what I am doing. You are learning to trust My love for you. You are also learning that your feelings have little to do with our relationship: I don't love you more when you feel close to Me, and I don't love you less when you feel far from Me.

Strength comes from resting in who I am. Believe I am all that I have said I am: Comforter, Shepherd, Friend, Burden-bearer, Protector and Shield, Fearless Warrior, Loving Parent, Trustworthy Counselor, the One who sees and loves you.

Perfect Love

Your love is complete in itself, isn't it, Lord. It doesn't change according to my response or feelings. I am free to be just who I am with You, and Your complete love covers all of me.

Beloved, My perfect love casts out fear. I love you perfectly. There are no imperfections, impurities, or mixtures in My love for you. It is 100% perfect, 100% pure, so you can trust it—you can let down your guard and rest.

Where My perfect love leads you, it is safe to follow. What My perfect love shows you, it is safe to see and receive. There is nothing My love for you cannot face. You are held secure in My love. My love embraces all of you and rejects no part. My love makes you whole.

Relax in My love. It is not fragile. It cannot be damaged or broken. My love is an unquenchable fire that feeds itself and needs no outside fuel to keep it going. Because My love is self-sustaining, you need not fear that your ups and downs will change My love for you.

Love Unchanging

I'm so glad that when I come to You, Lord, I can be confident You haven't changed towards me. People, myself included, are so changeable in our feelings for one another. I know that's just part of being human and imperfect, but it does make Your unchangeable love all the more precious.

I don't feel indulged or spoiled by Your love. You hold me to honesty before You. You don't let me fool myself or You about what's really going on inside of me. My heart has begun to flourish in Your honest, straightforward love. You see me as I really am and yet You love me extravagantly, passionately, persistently. And in Your unchangeable and perfect love I am free!

Beloved, did you know that even as you marvel and take delight in Me, I take great delight in you and am proud of you? If I were to tell you all that is in My heart for you, you wouldn't be able to receive it, but know that it is there waiting to be unwrapped—the gift of My love.

It is our love for one another, daughter, that will sustain you. You are Mine, and I am yours. This you can always depend on. This will never fail you. Love is the fuel that will keep you going. Do not neglect love—live in it, walk in it, depend on it, rest in it.

ENTER IN ...

The Lord your God is with you, he is mighty to save. He will take great delight in you, he will quiet you with his love, he will rejoice over you with singing.

—Zephaniah 3:17

Take a moment and rest in God's love for you. Lift your face to Him. Open your heart.

Just as a rose responds to the sun by opening its petals into full bloom, so our hearts were created to open to God and thrive on the love He pours out on us.

So for these moments, put aside any doubts or fears you have and just bask in God's priceless gift—His unconditional love for you.

CHAPTER 3

Belonging

~❧~

SHE WAS NEVER quite quick enough with him. His eyes found their way past her defenses and into her heart before she knew her mask had slipped. Although it was happening more frequently, she still wasn't comfortable with it—this uncanny knack he had for seeing right inside her.

She turned her eyes from his kind but knowing gaze and, slipping her mask back into place, rejoined the group. It was extremely unsettling to be a part of this gathering, but she knew it was expected of her.

Looking through the eye slits of her carefully crafted mask, she shuddered as she searched the faces of those around her. Though many in number, they wore identical masks. Their cold, unseeing eyes looked right through her, making her question, as she had many times before, if she were invisible. Stern, unsmiling mouths spoke unintelligible words that seemed nevertheless to demand a response from her.

She moved among them, her smiling mask in place, feeling frightened and bewildered. That she deserved this treatment she never questioned, but her instinct for self-preservation overcame all sense of duty. She began to look in desperation for a place to hide.

In rising panic her eyes searched the room for a way of escape, until she saw him. Their eyes locked. He moved quickly through the crowd and soon stood before her. His eyes pierced to the depths of her. It felt as if he reached into the core of her being and gripped some cringing thing he found there. With gentle, unrelenting strength he drew it from her, casting it aside. Then reaching out, he removed her mask.

She would relive this moment many times in the days to come, telling everyone who would listen that it had felt like a dam breaking within her. The swirling, rushing water had quickly filled her and then overflowed in rivers of tears down her face.

Unmasked, she looked with new eyes at the beloved face before her. How kind and compassionate he was!

Finally, dreading it, yet compelled to do so, she turned her eyes from his to the faces around them. Amazed at first, and then with dawning understanding, she looked from face to face. Each one was unique. The masks were gone. There were smiling faces, serious faces, curious, preoccupied, happy, sad, distracted faces—faces that held the promise of friendship, and those that didn't.

With clear, unmasked vision she looked with wonder and a rising sense of belonging at those around her—at the uncovered faces of her family.

Without a doubt, the area of life that has been the most challenging for me is that of relating to others—God included. As I look back on my life, I see that there have been experiences that contributed to this.

We were a military family and moved frequently. Being on the shy side, I found it more and more difficult to be the "new kid" in school. I would no sooner make a friend or two, than it was time to move. I always knew I would probably never see those friends again. "Out of sight, out of mind" became a way to deal with the loss of people in my life. Over the years, this pattern taught me to let go of people easily and not to expect relationships to last. I built walls of self-protection around my heart that led to patterns of fear and distrust. Eventually I began to misinterpret my sense of aloneness as rejection.

As I have already mentioned, my family's relational skills left much to be desired as well. Although we lived together, we didn't know how to listen to or encourage one another. Life was lonely, and the feeling of rejection grew strong, deep roots in me.

When I became a Christian, a few things changed overnight. I had a desire to read the Bible. The swearing I was getting pretty good at stopped. And I knew without a doubt that Jesus had come into my heart.

Life was good. God loved me.

But I soon discovered that along with this new relationship with God came a whole new family—God's family—and He wanted me to be a part of it. I didn't know it at the time, but I had many deep, festering wounds in my heart that would make learning to be a part of God's family a very painful process.

I had so much to learn about what it means to love and be loved.

Dare to Love

Lord, relating to others is like walking through a minefield: you never know when something will explode in your face. This is the hardest thing You have ever asked me to do—to be vulnerable to people. It scares me to death. No one knows better than You what giving yourself to people can cost. But I love You, Lord, and I want to please You, so I will follow You into the minefield. Please show me where to step, and make Your footsteps big and plain for me to follow. I'm very clumsy with people. Teach me the way of love.

Daughter, My love is not weak, sentimental, or superficial, and neither must yours be. If I am to love through you, you must be willing to let go of your idea that if you love others, you will be loved in return. That isn't always the case. What I hold you accountable for is your part, not the response you get. Do all you can to be a loving person and leave the results to Me.

Insecurity

Lord, please take away the fear and insecurity that hinder my relationships with others.

You are secure in My love. Pursue that relationship above all others, and then everything that causes such fear in you will come into proper perspective. Fear, insecurity, and rejection have wounded you. I want to heal your heart with My love. Rejection cannot hurt you when your heart is secure in My love for you.

Self-Acceptance

Sometimes it hurts to be me. Change me, Lord!

Beloved, why do you want to change so badly? Is it all right for you to be a little awkward and shy? Can you accept that about yourself if it never changes? If you will accept yourself, you will find that others feel more comfortable with you. Self-rejection is a denial of who you are—who I've created you uniquely to be. It is destructive and it is sin, daughter. The opposite of self-rejection is acceptance, and it has to begin with you.

Part of the Body

I want to love and serve You with others, Lord, but I don't seem to fit in very well.

Be released from the need to fit in, child. I am the one you need to fit in with, and I will fit you in where I want you.

Beloved, you need others. No one part can function alone. Being a part of the body is not optional for you. You may not pull away when you feel hurt. The body is designed to heal itself and nurture each part to health. You will never be a strong part if you pull away in times of pain. Life is in the body. Health is in the body. So don't pull away, draw in.

Rejection Hurts

Lord, I feel sick and insecure knowing there is someone who disapproves of me. I want to be understood, to vindicate myself in this situation. But I also know I'm trapped in an old, familiar way of thinking that says if people disapprove of me, there is something very wrong with me that they see and I don't. And that always leads to self-rejection and then this feeling of hopelessness. Please help me, Lord, to break out of this dead-end thinking.

Here's the truth, daughter. You are Mine, and I am yours. Nothing will ever separate you from My love. Know that you are secure in My perfect love for you. People are entitled to their opinions of you. Sometimes they will be right and sometimes wrong. They are imperfect, just as you are imperfect.

But others' opinions of you don't affect My opinion of you. I don't think better of you if you are liked by everyone and less if you are disliked. My love is based on the truth. It is rock-solid, unshakeable. You are the object of My perfect love, child, and that will never change.

So you are free to mix and mingle with others. Some will like, even love, you; others will not. That's okay. You are secure in My love.

When you offend others—and you will— ask for forgiveness, and then keep your heart open before Me so I can cleanse it and free you from a guilty conscience and the insecurity it causes. When others offend you—and they will—forgive them, and keep your heart open before Me so I can cleanse and strengthen it.

The more secure you become in My unshakeable love for you, the more resilient your heart will be. Perfect love casts out the fear of others' disapproval and rejection.

Differences on Display

Walking through a park, my husband and I joined several others at the edge of a pond, where we witnessed a sad struggle. An injured white bird was trying with great difficulty to stay balanced in the water. A group of mallards had formed a ring around the injured bird, also watching its struggle. Although it was heart-wrenching, later that day the Lord let me know He had something to teach me through it.

What do you want me to understand from what we saw, Lord?

Not everyone fits in with the group—perhaps due to injury, perhaps just because they seem different. The injured bird was lovely even though it was different from the others. You admired its beauty and felt compassion for its injury. You have compassion for the helpless and injured, daughter, because you have been both. Rather than rejecting yourself for what makes you different, let Me have it and turn it into something lovely.

Be content with characteristics that make you feel different from those around you. Don't long to belong. Live your life for Me. Let Me bring out the loveliness I see. There will always be enemies; there will always be admirers. I haven't asked you to be a chameleon, changing to please others or to fit in out of self-protection. Like the bird, I have asked you to live your life, your unique life, just as it really is: differences and injuries on display, vulnerable to those who pass by, but never out of My sight—never out of My loving care.

Yes, Lord. And please care for that poor little creature and protect it from further injury. Provide a place of refuge and help it in its helplessness.

That little creature you feel so much compassion for has brought Me glory, and so will you.

ENTER IN ...

Relationships with others give us some of the greatest joy we can experience as well as the deepest pain.

May I suggest that you spend a few moments recalling your experiences of both—joy and pain. Then thank God for the people who have given your heart a home, those who have increased your sense of belonging.

Bring to Him the relationships that have caused you pain. Lay them at His feet and ask Him to heal your broken heart. Choose to forgive those who have hurt you, and keep on forgiving until your heart is truly free. God is the expert on healing broken hearts, and He will delight in doing that for you.

If you have developed unhealthy or destructive ways of coping with emotional pain or of relating to others, acknowledge that openly to the Lord, who loves you. Make a choice to turn from those ways, and ask our all-powerful God to teach you new ways—His ways that lead to life.

This kind of change rarely happens overnight, but it *will* happen if you stay in the transformation process with God.

CHAPTER 4

Learning to Listen

❧

TAKE UP YOUR pen, and I will speak to you.

The first time I heard those words, I had just told the Lord that I wanted to be able to hear His voice clearly, as clearly as Abraham heard Him in a passage I had just read in Genesis. But even though I had asked, I couldn't believe God had really answered, so I ignored His instruction to take up a pen and went on my way.

Several months passed, and again the words came: *Take up your pen, and I will speak to you.* This time I thought perhaps it really was God I was hearing, and if it was, then I should obey. I began asking Him questions and then writing down His answers. Even as I wrote what I was hearing, I struggled to believe that God would speak to me. But since it seemed I had His attention, I decided to hold nothing back. I asked Him question after question about things I had struggled with for most of my years as a Christian. I had known God for a long time, but this was the first two-way conversation I had ever had with Him.

As I reread that first conversation, which follows, I'm amazed at His patience. Love Himself was knocking on my heart's door, but my main concern was to have Him fill out my questionnaire! What kindness! What love! But, however rocky, this began the greatest adventure of my life: learning to listen to God.

God Speaks My Language

Take up your pen, and I will speak to you. There are many things we must talk about.

Lord, am I talking to myself, or is this really You?

Don't analyze yourself right now—this is not you talking to yourself, but Me. Why wouldn't I speak to you? Do you want that more than I do?

Child, how can I show you how real I am and how real I want to be in your life? What will you believe of Me? Will you let Me love you? How can I show you how precious you are to Me?

Lord, I'm having a very difficult time understanding something I saw, and it's breaking my heart. It was a picture in a magazine of a little girl dying of starvation while a vulture waited nearby. God, it hurts so much to know about the suffering of the children in our world.

The little girl is with Me now. Don't seal yourself off from hurt, daughter. That is what makes you tender. Let the tears flow.

But, Lord, are the sin and suffering in our world out of control?

What are you asking, daughter? Are the sin and suffering out of My control? Are they being controlled by Satan?

I'm sorry, Lord. But why do You allow suffering like this?

Daughter, is your grief greater than Mine? It is because of the suffering that I died—to give hope, to birth life out of death.

Yes, there is pain, but there is also joy. You won't fully appreciate the joy that awaits you if you don't feel the pain of today. Suffering and pain aren't a virtue, but they are a present reality in the world. They will crush you if you don't share them with Me. Don't blame Me for the suffering, praise Me in the midst of it, and ask Me to redeem it. I'm the Redeemer, the Changer, the Fixer of the broken things. Don't question My integrity and love. Even though you can't fully understand, you know enough of My love to trust Me.

Lord, what about the depression and inner struggles I experience?

My grace is sufficient. My strength is made perfect in weakness. Your weaknesses are not My limitations. I could remove them in a minute. Would

You trust Me more then? My grace is sufficient; learn the meaning of this. I am pleased when you exercise faith in Me during difficult times. Listen to Me closely, daughter. The struggles in this life will not all end, but I will reveal Myself to you and through you in the midst of the struggle.

What about my fears, Lord?

Don't own fear; use it. Let it teach you to be courageous.

How can fear teach me to be courageous?

Insist that fear obey you and that it submit to Me, the Lord. Is it stronger than I? Can fear thwart My purposes? The goal isn't for you to overcome your weaknesses, but that you recognize who I am in the midst of your weaknesses. They do not limit Me.

And relationships? You know my tendency to isolate and not develop many close relationships.

This will be hard for you to receive, beloved, but it's important for you to know: I am not disappointed in you. Do all you know to be a loving person, and leave the rest with Me. Our relationship is precious to Me. Receive My friendship. You need Me. I know the way of loneliness, and only I can keep you from being overwhelmed by it.

Loneliness has, in part, made you who you are. It's been one of My tools in your life. It's not a friend, but neither is it an enemy. It just is, and I have used it for My purposes. Would you long for Me so, had you not known loneliness? Would we have had such precious times together without it? Love people, but belong to Me. You are Mine, and no one can care for you as tenderly as I do. When you feel unloved or misunderstood, remember that is My responsibility. It won't hurt Me, but it will hurt you.

Your weaknesses are not My limitations. Let them be useful to Me. Don't hide them in shame. Stand with them before Me, and watch what I will do!

Over the next several weeks God continued to counsel me as I struggled with issues related to listening to His voice. I knew that God speaks to His people by His Spirit, through His written Word, but this was something new for me and a bit scary. (I should say here that I am not talking about hearing God's *audible* voice, but rather the quiet words He impresses on our hearts by His Spirit.) I had no trouble believing that others heard God speak to them, but that He would speak to *me* in everyday language about *my* concerns was a stretch of faith I wasn't sure I was ready to take. But my hunger for greater intimacy with God slowly overcame my fear of presumption, and I continued to spend time with God with a pen in hand.

I believe God speaks to us frequently and in a great variety of ways: through His written Word, His creation, thoughts the Holy Spirit impresses on our hearts, the counsel of others, and the peace and confidence He gives when we seek to know His will—just to mention a few.

The Bible, of course, must always be the standard by which we measure anything we hear. When I sense I'm hearing from God, I've discovered that unless I write down what I am hearing, I have no way of remembering it long enough to test it by time and the written Word. The words that prove over time to have life and weight to them are the ones I hang onto and have found to be life-changing.

Following are additional words of God's counsel to me that are related to hearing His voice.

My Sheep Hear My Voice

Daughter, I would like to visit with you. I know it's hard for you to believe that I enjoy your company, but it is true. You are my beloved daughter, but you are also My friend, and friends share their lives with one another. Your joys are My joys, your concerns are My concerns.

Lord, please help me to better discern Your voice these days. I don't want to be saying nice things to myself, thinking it's You I hear, and sometimes it's very hard to know the difference.

My sheep hear My voice, beloved. Remember that. I'm talking to you as a friend and that troubles you because it doesn't sound as spiritual as you think God should sound. I was a carpenter—remember? I talked about ordinary things every day, things that make up the stuff of everyday life. Because I

*experienced the ordinary in My life on earth, I understand the ordinary things
in your life: meeting deadlines, relationships with others, caring for your
family, and your worries and fears. I understand all of these things. Nothing
is too small or unimportant for My interest. You are Mine and I am yours
and we live life together. This is the way I planned it. I never intended for
people to visit Me one day a week and shut Me out of the rest of their days.
This grieves Me and hinders them from entering into real life.*

Lord, on the one hand I want to believe You are this personal,
interested, and approachable, but on the other hand, something in me
feels I should keep You at a holy distance. I'm a little confused by this,
because it's forcing me to think about You so differently.

*Daughter, you are beginning to understand how real I am, that I am
not an idea to pick up or discard according to your mood. I am here, I am
God, and I am your friend. The more time we spend together, the more
familiar you will become with My ways, and the more I will be able to
share with you.*

Presumption?

Lord, am I being presumptuous expecting You to speak to me?

*Beloved, you have asked Me to teach you to pray. How will you know
what to pray unless you learn to hear My voice? This is not something
unusual. I speak to My people. But you struggle with the same unbelief that
has dulled many others' ears to My voice.*

*Will you turn away, daughter, or will you press in and take hold of that
to which I have called you?*

To Listen or Not to Listen

These are interesting days. I waiver between excitement over God's
speaking to me in a way that I can hear Him, and unbelief that He would
do that. Is it really Him speaking, or just my own thoughts?

However, if this *is* the Lord teaching me to hear His voice, then
suddenly He's much more real, and I have to be more real. Till now I
could read my Bible, pray a little, and then go on my way. Now, however,
I have to reckon with a relationship where He's in charge.

Will my time with Him be something that I fit into my schedule, or will He want my schedule to be directed by my time with Him? It's so much easier to have a "quiet time" than to meet with a real, live God who wants to talk to me.

It seems my need for control in life has even affected my relationship with God, and He has let me get away with it for so long! What patience!

Lord, I feel a struggle going on in me. I feel frustrated. I want to get up from this table and get on with the day. I think I want to hear You speak to me, but maybe I'm too used to the old way, with me seeming to be in charge. Maybe I don't want to hear You as much as I've said I do.

We will work on this matter of control together, daughter. Your weaknesses are not My limitations. No stronghold is greater than Me and My purposes in your life. That is why you must get to know Me. You will see that I am trustworthy.

Listening—An Adventure of Faith

How can I trust what I hear, Lord? What if I make a mistake?

Frequent listening will attune your ears to My voice. I will entrust to you what you are willing and ready to hear. With listening comes responsibility to act and obey. I don't speak to deaf ears. I speak to those who are eager and hungry to know My ways and obey them.

Put aside your grid that filters out all that you don't understand. My ways are not your ways, nor are your thoughts My thoughts. I must be able to speak to you freely, and you must be willing to listen by faith. I will take responsibility for keeping you on track, if you will come to Me in faith.

The Written Word and Hearing His Voice

God's written Word, the Bible, has been a powerful tool in my life. I find the more time I spend in the written Word, the more likely I am to hear God speak to me. I believe that a vital part of hearing God's voice is a growing knowledge of and obedience to His written Word. I'm so grateful for God's servants who teach me the Word, and for those who have encouraged me to memorize portions of His Word. But I find I can be unbalanced in my approach to the Bible, by either neglecting relationship with God Himself when I read or study His Word, or by ignoring His Word during times of just relating and listening to His voice. I desperately need both. Here is what He has said to me on this subject:

Daughter, your study of My Word will never take the place of your need for Me, for I am a Person and, like you, I long for relationship. You will never outgrow your need to listen to My voice, beloved. This is something you must not let slip away.

But this is a season of study for you, and I am your Teacher. You cannot understand My Word without My personal involvement and instruction. So open your Bible and study books, and invite My Spirit to teach you. We will fellowship in study, even as we fellowship in conversation. Ask Me questions as you read, and listen for My answers. Don't stop listening for My voice just because you are studying. I will teach you to do both.

My Word is food for your soul and a tool for your work. My Word is powerful. You are seeing the effects of My Word in your struggle with fear. Fear and truth cannot coexist; one will grow stronger and defeat the other. If fear is fed, it wins the battle. If truth is fed, it wins. Feeding yourself big doses of truth will supplant fear. This is lasting deliverance!

Time to Listen

I'm sorry I've neglected spending time with You lately, Lord.

Daughter, you have not neglected Me. Your longing for Me is prayer, and I have heard. Life will not always allow you long, uninterrupted time with Me, as much as we would both enjoy that. Continue to seek Me as you go about your everyday business of serving and caring for others. Fellowship with Me in the routine of your day. This pleases Me greatly and will train your heart in its ability to hear My voice among many distractions.

But we do need time together, beloved, and so we will find it. Just as your relationship with your husband is sweetened when nurtured by time alone, so it is with our relationship. Does your husband reject you when life keeps you both so busy you can't spend much time together? Of course not. Neither do I reject you. But loved ones need time to talk and enjoy each other's company. You grow sad and lonely when you stay away too long, beloved, so we will find time to spend together.

More than Words

I love Your words to me, Lord. Thank You! Please increase my capacity to hear Your voice.

If you will listen, I will speak to you. I long to share My heart and My thoughts with you—much more than you want to listen. I am increasing your faith and ability to hear Me. But seek Me for Myself, not just for My words. You are much more than ears to Me, and I must be more than just words to you.

I am your Lord, your Heavenly Father, your Friend, and your Counselor. I am all around you. I am within you. I am your life. Know that when you talk to Me you are talking to a being with intellect, humor, creativity, wisdom, compassion, understanding, and sorrow. All that you have known, I have known and experienced. I am more real than you know.

ENTER IN ...

Jesus, Living Word of God, You are my life! I desperately need Your counsel and comfort, but my days are filled with distractions and demands that seem more urgent than time spent with You.

See my weakness, Lord. Out of Your mercy please kindle a fresh fire of love and longing in my heart for You. Increase my hunger for Your presence and Your word; and teach me, Lover of My Soul, to hear Your voice however You choose to speak to me.

Thank You, Living Word, for hearing and answering this cry of my heart.

Your beloved

CHAPTER 5

Darkness

PART 1: WALKING IN THE DARK

I'M SO GRATEFUL for David's honesty in the Psalms. He told God how he really felt. By making David's inner struggles and feelings a part of His written Word, I believe God was validating this aspect of our humanness.

My melancholy nature and tendency toward depression have driven me to God more times than I can count. The temptation to give up, feel hopeless, and lose my sense of purpose and direction has been a common theme in my conversations with God. But in the dark times when God has seemed distant, He has reminded me time and again: *I will never forsake you, you are Mine.*

Trust

Lord, I feel like I'm stumbling around in the dark these days.

Then trust Me in the dark. It's easy to trust when the sun is shining and all is going well, but faith is required to trust Me when it is dark. Say with David: "How long, O Lord?" yet also say, "But I trust in Your unfailing love" (Psalm 13:1, 5).

I understand your weariness, but you must not give up. Learn to walk in the dark with Me.

Never Alone

Lord, at times like this I feel so cut off from You.

I surround you, beloved—front, back, below, above. You live and move and have your being in Me. I am also within you. From the inside to the outside, I am with you. There is no place you can go from My Spirit, no place where My presence will not be with you.

I have bound you to Myself with cords of everlasting and unfailing love. Do not fear being left in the darkness. I will never forsake you. You are Mine.

> If I say, Surely the darkness shall cover me and the night shall be [the only] light about me, even the darkness hides nothing from You, but the night shines as the day; the darkness and the light are both alike to You.
> —Psalm 139:11–12 AMPLIFIED

When the Loving Feelings Are Gone

Forgive me, Lord, for not loving You more.

You don't need to manufacture feelings for Me to please Me. I see into your heart, and My place there is secure. I understand your ups and downs and accept you as you are. You belong to Me; you are My precious child.

Your feelings will come and go, daughter, but you are being strengthened to stand by faith. Acting on faith is what pleases Me, not responding to good feelings. Your walk with Me must be based on your sure knowledge of My character, not your feelings. This is foundational to all we will do together.

Sunshine and Shadow

Lord, I don't like myself when I feel like this. Surely this can't be Your will for me.

Beloved, just as the sun and the clouds are part of My will, so your light, carefree times as well as the darker times are part of My will. I allow both and use both for My purposes. The constant in these illustrations is the powerful sun behind the clouds. Though I may be hidden from your sight for a time, I have not changed. Never fear following Me, My daughter.

> Who is among you who [reverently] fears the Lord, who obeys the voice of His Servant, yet who walks in darkness and deep trouble and has no shining splendor [in his heart]? Let him rely on, trust in, and be confident in the name of the Lord, and let him lean upon and be supported by his God.
> —Isaiah 50:10 AMPLIFIED

Overcome

Worry and fear have overcome me, Lord!

Your worries and fears are all known to Me. Worry and fear "with" Me. Be conscious of My presence right in the midst of them. I turn darkness into light. I give understanding and insight. I know what to do. Bring it all with you when you enter My presence.

Praying in the Dark

Lord, teach me to pray and follow You in the Spirit no matter how oppressed or depressed my emotions and mind may be. But is this possible, Lord? Is it possible to serve and please You in the spiritual realm at the same time my mind and emotions seem so clouded and dull? Are the only prayers that count the ones accompanied by fervor and feelings of faith, by anointed words, and a sense of Your presence? What about the times like now when my mind and emotions seem to be on holiday somewhere without me and all I can do is long for You and better days?

Daughter, allow no self-pity here, but pursue these thoughts, for they are very important.

I hear both your prayers of fervor and the unspoken longings in your heart. Both are prayer. More importantly, I see you, beloved, and know you. And what I know goes deeper than any words you could say. Rest in

My knowledge of you. You don't need to impress Me with prayers; I see your heart. Speak out of your heart, or be silent.

Labyrinth of the Soul

Matthew 11:28–30 says, "Come to me, all you who are weary and burdened, and I will give you rest. Take my yoke upon you and learn from me, for I am gentle and humble in heart and you will find rest for your souls."

Lord, I so rarely feel at rest. What am I yoked to that causes me to feel weary and burdened? I have felt this way many times before, and I must hear from You if I am to grow beyond this point. I'm asking You for breakthroughs in understanding and in believing and receiving Your love. I want to be yoked to You alone and to find rest for my soul.

Beloved, follow the promptings of your heart and have patience with the process of learning and understanding My ways in your life. I'm not impatient or dissatisfied with your growth progress. The danger is in your believing that I am. That will cause you to draw away from Me. Growth isn't something you do on your own and then show Me to get a pat on the head. Growth and rest come as you bring all your struggles to Me and face them honestly with Me. Let Me bear the burden of the inner struggle with you. Be yoked to Me in the battle for your life and My purposes.

But I'm ashamed, Lord, that I'm still stuck here, having to work on me rather than being free to give my life away for others and their needs.

You are doing both. You will never outgrow the need to work on you. Growth implies change, stretching, becoming. You won't one day arrive at maturity and then be free to give your life away for others. You will always be doing both simultaneously. The more you participate in the inner transformation I am working in you, the more you will have to give away.

Never be ashamed of being a work in process. Life lived with Me is dynamic: moving, changing, filling, emptying, growing, stretching, uprooting, planting. The place of peace and rest is never a stagnant, "having-arrived" place.

Peace and rest come from knowing and experiencing the fact that at the very core of your being we are inseparably united to one another. I am the home, the rock, the solid place, the anchor of your soul. From that secure place, we then move out together to face the adventures of the soul: the growing, changing, stretching, and, yes, the waiting, questioning, and suffering of the soul.

So I'm not "stuck," Lord?

You will feel stuck when you wander out on your own into the labyrinth of your soul. It's easy to lose your way and become confused. Keep reminding yourself that you are not alone—that you are with Me always, and I know where I'm going. I will never go back on My promise to guide you, teach you, and instruct you in My way for you. Every way but Mine leads to a dead end, so stay close to Me, and let Me lead you.

Merriam Webster's Collegiate Dictionary gives this definition of the word labyrinth: "(a) a place constructed of or full of intricate passageways and blind alleys (b) a maze (as in a garden) formed by paths separated by high hedges. (2) Something extremely complex or tortuous in structure, arrangement, or character: intricacy, perplexity."

That sounds like life to me, and the inner life especially. Forgive me, Lord, for the time I waste wandering around *leaning on my own understanding* as Proverbs 3:5 puts it. Here's my hand once again, Lord. Please lead me on this journey through the labyrinth of my soul.

I Believe!

> Blessed is she who has believed that what the Lord has said
> to her will be accomplished!
> —Luke 1:45

Lord, I give up all my expectations of how I will *feel* if I am in Your will and close to You. Today I feel dull and distant, but You are faithful and unchanging, and I rest all the weight of my life on You. I love You, Lord. It's because of Your *trustworthiness* that I am confident, because of Your *love* that I feel secure, because of Your *faithfulness* that I will not worry and fret, because of Your *mercy* and *grace* that I will not fear, because of Your *power* that I will not give up, because of Your *promises* that I will hope.

Sometimes I feel like that "leaning wall" and "tottering fence" mentioned in Psalm 62:3—so unstable in myself. But You, Lord, are my *Rock*, my *Salvation*, my *Fortress*, and I will not be shaken. My hope comes from You.

"Find rest, O my soul, in God alone..." (Psalm 62:5)—not in good feelings, not in success, not in pleasing circumstances, but in *God* and all He has revealed Himself to be.

Lord, You remain the same in spite of feelings, ups and downs of ministry, spiritual highs and lows, and changes in circumstances. My security and hope are *in You!*

PART 2: OUT OF THE DUNGEON

She sat in the damp gloom of her cell, considering the object in her hand. That it was an object of significance she had no doubt, but why it was significant eluded her clouded mind.

The call startled her up from the depths of her musings: "The King is in residence! All is well!"

The familiar words echoed off the walls of her prison. A herald, sent from the palace courts in the floors above, made his way along the corridors of the dungeon each day at this time. His message never changed, and it never failed to produce a volley of grumbling and complaining from the occupants of the dark cells he passed. "All is well, indeed! The King's not sitting in this hellhole! Go away! And take your fairytale with you!"

Most days she joined the angry chorus of resentment, but not this day.

She watched as the sliver of light that had entered her cell with the herald's words began to diffuse the gloom that surrounded her. Then, as if parting a heavy curtain, the light made a path through the fog in her mind.

Light…she remembered light… Yes, the King himself had come to her prison door one day. She remembered… He had unlocked the door and stepped inside. The light had almost blinded her. Then he had led her out of her cell, down the long corridor, up many stairs…

Fully alert now, she remembered the beautiful days in the courts of the King. His face came before her—his strong, kind face. He had spoken many things to her in those days, life-giving words of love, joy, and peace. But he had also warned her of the dungeon and its power to deceive even those who lived in the courts of the King. Then he had placed something in her hand and said, "No prison door can hold you that I have once opened."

She glanced down at the object in her hand. Of course! Rising to her feet, she approached the door of her cell, and taking the key, inserted it into the lock. Her prison door opened. Retrieving the key, she stepped out into the corridor and joined the herald in joyfully proclaiming, "The King is in residence! All is well!"

Sometimes the darkness I experience requires a different response than persevering in faith and trusting God to sustain me in dark times. Sometimes He asks me to fight for the freedom He won for me at the cross. This is especially true when the darkness is a result of my neglecting the truth and allowing lies and old patterns of thinking and feeling to creep in. The devil is quick to take advantage of those times, and I can find myself sitting in a place as dark as the dungeon in the story.

God frequently reminds me that He has set me free from the power of old lies. He has put the key of truth in my hand, and He will empower me to use it against the lies when they seek to imprison me once again. But I must use the key and refuse to be made a prisoner. That is *never* easy to do. The devil's lies can come with a powerful delusion and can seem more real than memories of freedom.

When the lies are old and have worn deep grooves in my thinking, the Lord has often used another person to bring exposure and shine His light of truth. But I've been amazed many times by how quickly the darkness will lift when I finally take a stand with the truth and resist the devil.

I love this portion of Psalm 129: "They have greatly oppressed me from my youth—let Israel say—they have greatly oppressed me from my youth, but they have not gained the victory over me. Plowmen have plowed my back and made their furrows long. But the Lord is righteous; he has cut me free from the cords of the wicked."

Praise His name!

Housecleaning

Jesus, be Lord and King of my heart. Rule and reign over all the fears and troubling things that torment me.

Yes! Let's clean house! These musty, dirty things don't belong here in My home. I'm sweeping out fear and worry. Insecurity and rejection—leave My home! Hopelessness—get out!

Now let's open the windows and let in the Breath of Life. Come, Breath of Life. Blow through every chamber to cleanse and restore to life what has been choked or suffocated. Breathe in deeply, daughter, welcoming My life-giving Spirit.

Jesus, I am Your home. You live in me. Thank You, wonderful Savior, for the precious picture of us sharing a home in my heart. Somehow it changes everything. With You at home in me, there's no place for the old, lonely, empty feelings. Thank You, wonderful Lord!

Is the struggle over, Lord?

Have courage, daughter. The battle isn't over, but the victory is ours! I know of your weariness, but you must continue to stand in the truth.

Yes, Lord.

You, O Lord, keep my lamp burning; my God turns my darkness into light.

—Psalm 18:28

ENTER IN ...

Then you will know the truth and the truth will set you free.

—John 8:32

This is a wonderful promise, but I've discovered that in order to receive God's life-changing truth, I must first allow Him to expose the lies I have believed.

Painful life experiences can lead us to many wrong conclusions that distort the truth about God, about ourselves, and about others. Of course, willfulness and rebellion can also keep us from seeing what is true. But whatever the cause, God's desire is to lead us out of the darkness of deception and into the freedom and light of truth.

Is there an area of your life where you know you are not free? Ask the Lord to reveal to you the lies that are robbing you of the abundant life He has planned for you. If the lies are old and deeply rooted, He may use a wise and trusted friend or counselor to help you see them.

Write the lies down. Ask God to show you the truth that refutes those lies. It may come from a variety of sources: Bible passages, the counsel of His Spirit, a godly friend, a wise counselor. Write down the truth and keep it handy.

Whenever you find yourself feeling, thinking, or acting in the old ways, based on lies, call out to God for His help and power. Tell Him what is happening (He already knows, of course, but He wants you to invite Him into the situation). Then speak the truth, and renounce the lies. With the unbeatable combination of God's power at work in you and your willingness to be changed and freed, you will soon find yourself spending more time in the light and less and less in the darkness.

Be patient with the process of developing new ways of feeling, thinking, and acting. God is patient, and no one is cheering you on more than He is!

CHAPTER 6

Grace!

THE GRACE GOD shows me as I stumble along with Him never fails to amaze me. His kindness continually melts my heart. My human nature understands the "eye for an eye" approach much better than it does unearned, undeserved favor. To expect disapproval and condemnation and receive only grace has healed my heart time and time again.

The Lord often speaks to me by impressing a picture on my mind. He showed me a funny one to illustrate how He views the imperfections in my life: the unfinished business that can trip me up and make me ashamed of myself. As He and I walked along together, He had His arm over my shoulder. We were having a wonderful time in close communion. The picture conveyed His love and acceptance of me. Then I saw the tin cans. Noisy tin cans, attached by long strings, dragged along behind me. It wasn't a flattering picture!

But with the picture, came understanding of its meaning. I realized that the tin cans represented the unfinished business of my life—the wrong attitudes and motives, the destructive thought patterns, sinful reactions, and unhealed emotions—the areas where I may know the truth, but haven't been fully changed by the truth.

Sometimes I'm unaware of what I still drag along. As David says in Psalm 19:12, "Who can discern his errors? Forgive my hidden faults." Other times, I'm very aware of my imperfections, and they distress me greatly. My mind can be in full agreement with the Lord's way, but I may still respond to emotions and broken parts that tell me something very different. When this happens, my tendency is to disqualify myself and want to hide in shame from the Lord and others.

But the Lord showed me through this picture that He loves me and wants me by His side always. Even though He is very aware of the noisy "tin cans" of my life, they do not disqualify me from walking with Him in close fellowship and service.

What He requires of me is that I honestly acknowledge my weaknesses and sins to Him, and agree with Him about them. Then, as I walk along with Him, He can do the exposing, washing, healing, delivering, and transforming miracles He longs to do.

The tin cans will eventually drop away, or be recycled into something useful, and our walk together will become less "noisy." However, He frequently reminds me that I will always need a Savior—for this He came.

Ashes to Glory

Lord, I fear I've disappointed You. I want to be strengthened to love and follow You consistently, but like Cinderella, here I am—dressed in my rags again and sitting in the ashes.

Beloved, no one loves a Cinderella story more than I do. I delight in turning ashes to glory, sadness to joy, weakness to strength. I AM ABLE. You are weak—I am strong. You must learn to depend on Me—I am dependable. I didn't draw you to Myself because of your strengths, I drew you because I love you. I knew your weaknesses when I called you, and they are only a limitation if you rely on yourself.

The Prince has come to rescue you. Now rise up and come with Me. Leave your fears behind in the ash heap, where they belong. The slipper I bring fits only you, and I make no mistakes.

Muddy Feet

When I see what's really in my heart at times, Lord, I feel so ashamed. Shouldn't I be better than this by now?

Beloved, I am your Father, and I know My child. Come to Me and do not fear, for My love is pure and has power to overcome all impurities. Never let shame keep you from Me. I understand your every thought, motive, and temptation, and none of them put Me off or offend Me. You are My precious child, and I want you to come to Me just as you are. Just as a little child can track mud in the house without losing a good parent's love, so you are welcome in My presence with any "mud" you may pick up along the way. In My presence you are made clean.

Guilt

Lord, so much has changed in my life these days. I know I've withdrawn from You and am in survival mode. You must be so disappointed in me that I'm not dealing with life with more faith in You. I'm so sorry.

Beloved, don't let guilty feelings keep you away from Me. You have not disappointed Me. Nothing has changed in our relationship. What you are experiencing are normal human responses to change. I understand. Your neediness, your humanness draws compassion from Me, not harshness or disappointment. You are learning a new way to live life with Me. It won't happen quickly, but I am patient. We have all eternity ahead of us!

Receive My peace, My joy, dear one, and rest in My love for you. "… in quietness and trust is your strength" (Isaiah 30:15).

Your love and kindness have overwhelmed me once again, dear Lord and Friend. Thank You for the warmth melting the cold knot of anxiety in me.

Selfishness

Lord, I'm ashamed that so much of my time with You—even my praying—is self-centered. I seem incapable of forgetting myself. Why am I still so self-conscious after all You've done for me?

Daughter, leave this with Me. It's enough for you to recognize it. You have asked Me to purify you, and that is what I am doing. How I do it is up to Me. I don't want you groveling in self-blame and self-pity. I have told you many times that I AM ABLE to bring to completion what I have begun in you. I am your Lord. I have paid for all your sins. You are clean because I am the Righteous One who has forgiven and healed you. Your self-recrimination does you no good—neither does it honor Me.

When sin is exposed, acknowledge it, rejoice in who I am in you, and move on in victory. Give no foothold to the devil to fill you with needless guilt and shame. My power in you is greater than your sin nature. Saving and sanctifying you is My work, not yours. Delight and rejoice in Me and My righteousness. You will never be good enough to take pride in your own goodness.

I laughed and laughed with the Lord at this last comment. Then it struck me how much it cost Him to be able to say that. He paid everything to win for me this place of freedom to sometimes fail and sin and then start again without guilt and shame. Tears of deepest gratitude followed.

Searching for Sin

I have this sense that I'm not pleasing You, Lord, but I can't seem to put my finger on anything specific.

It's better if you let My Spirit do the heart-searching, beloved. That's My work, not yours. Your searching leads to condemnation; Mine leads to peace. So don't go looking for your faults. That is a work of the flesh and accomplishes nothing. Let peace rule your heart and rejoice in My favor.

Here I Go Again

It seems every time You use me in some good way, Lord, I'm tempted to be proud of myself and want the affirmation of others. Please help me to just keep serving and not get stuck in the struggle with pride.

I understand your concern, daughter, but you must not move on so quickly that you miss the joy of partnering with Me out of fear of pride.

I need to understand this better, Lord. I want to be a vessel You can use for Your purposes, but then I get so ashamed of all the foolish thoughts that accompany any victory or good thing You do.

Beloved, I'm not going to stop using you because you struggle with pride. I would be more concerned if you didn't grieve over it. But the bigger picture is what I am doing, and you have the privilege of having a part in it. Focus on that.

There will always be temptations to pride, but as your faith grows, you will be quicker to deal with them.

It is My joy to have you at My side. I'm not disappointed in you when you occasionally stumble and fall. The important thing is that you keep getting up and continuing on. Even your stumbling is part of your training. It teaches you dependence, it enables you to have compassion for others who are also stumbling, it defeats the lie that you have to be perfect to be accepted, and it is giving you a deep appreciation for the sacrifice My Son made on your behalf.

Don't let failure stop you. Be grateful for the cross, wash quickly, then look in My face, and get back in the joyful race.

True Repentance

I keep falling into the same old patterns, Lord—striving to prove myself, to feel important, to measure up well in comparison with others. Pride and self-focus stick to me like glue. I don't like this about myself, but I can't seem to do much better. Please forgive me.

My dear daughter, I do forgive you and assure you that I know your heart much better than you know yourself. I am not repulsed by what you are seeing more clearly about yourself. What pleases Me is your acknowledgment of sin and your desire to change. But repentance and self-condemnation are two different things. True repentance comes from love of Me. Self-condemnation comes from pride and disappointment in yourself. I will accept your repentance, but not your self-condemnation.

Will repentance change me, Lord?

Repentance puts the matter in My hands and waits patiently for Me. Self-condemnation is impatient and looks for results that feed the cycle of pride. If I can love you with all your faults and patiently teach you My ways, you must do the same. You must love yourself even though you are imperfect, and trust Me by being patient with My working in you to heal and change.

By turning your attention from worry about your imperfect self to the Perfect One who loves you, you will find rest for your soul.

Grace, love, and mercy are My ways. Walk in them, and you will please Me in every way.

Lord, thank You for Your patience with my humanity. I feel loved and understood by You and full of hope that the way I am now is not the way I will be if I keep walking with You.

From Darkness to Light

It was my birthday, and I was reflecting on my life—kind of a recap of the years. And although I had much to be grateful for, I realized I was very disappointed in myself. I saw many dips and valleys in my walk with God. So I asked Him, "Lord, how do *You* see my life?"

Beloved, I see your life as a light growing brighter with each passing year until you are in My presence and shine with My glory within and upon you.

And all the dark spots along the way, Lord?

What dark spots?

Sin, struggle, depression…

My eye misses nothing, beloved, but I am showing you My perspective of your life. Do you see all that My Son has done for you? I see the light, not the darkness. He took all the darkness into Himself as if it were His own and then poured out His blood so that I would see no dark spots when I look at you and consider your life. That's the truth you must live by. It will free you to live lighter and happier. Believe it. Practice it.

That seems too good to be true, Lord! Is this really You? Are you really saying that when You look at me You see only light? I have to see this in Your Word.

…my God turns my darkness into light.

—Psalm 18:28

The light of the righteous shines brightly.

—Proverbs 13:9

For you were once darkness, but now you are light in the Lord.

—Ephesians 5:8

Amazing, Lord! This is a fresh perspective for me. I've never seen it like this before. I am light in the Lord. I live in a Kingdom of Light. I live in the presence of Light Himself. God only sees light when He looks at me in Christ. How wonderfully and utterly amazing!

Truth of God, go deep now and set me free from error and deception. Make me shine, dear Light of the World, according to the truth!

ENTER IN ...

For it is by grace you have been saved, through faith—and
this not from yourselves, it is the gift of God—not by works,
so that no one can boast.

—Ephesians 2:8–9

God's grace is so foreign to my natural human ways that
from time to time I have to go back to the basics and give myself
a talking to. I remind myself:

This life is not about your trying to be good enough to
make up for your sin or impress God so He'll let you into His
heaven. And a list of good works will never be long enough
to earn God's or anyone else's approval. So just receive God's
forgiveness and approval as the astounding gifts that they
are. Jesus met the standard for you. He is fully approved by
God, and by faith in Him, you will be carried by His grace
right into heaven.

Now you are free to live your life for love's sake rather
than striving to earn your way. Now you can serve God out
of gratitude and have a sincere compassion for people rather
than having to prove yourself. God's grace frees you from
all condemnation.

Grace—we may not fully understand it, but it's worth
shouting about and doing a dance to hallelujahs!

Why not find a private place right now and give yourself
up to joy and thankfulness for the grace God has poured out
on you.

CHAPTER 7

Whom Do You Serve?

THIS TIME SHE had gone too far. This time she would pay the price.

It wasn't the first time she had ventured out on her own. Her desire to be useful often drove her out of the palace. She always tried to keep the lighted courts in view, but the cries from the darkness were so compelling that she felt she must respond.

She had been warned many times that she must not venture out unless by a direct invitation to follow her King. But the desire to be useful overcame all warnings.

Now, here she was—her legs severely injured by a fall and unable to move.

Lights from the palace courts taunted her. She could see them shining dimly through the darkness, an impossible distance away.

Overcome by regret, she lay in her pain, helpless and alone. She had failed him, and rather than being helpful, she had been foolish—as her crippled body testified.

Hopelessness welled up in her. She had brought this on herself. To expect help would be presumptuous. But how she longed for the King and the light of his courts.

The darkness pressed down upon her; her suffering was acute. Yet even more painful than her broken limbs was the pain of having to let go of her dreams—dreams of what she wanted to do for her King. One by one they passed before her, mocking her powerlessness to ever fulfill them.

How long she lay in the darkness, she did not know. But through the fog of her suffering she became aware of arms reaching down to her. Hands marked by scars lifted her.

Gently, so gently, the King carried her. Into his courts he brought her.

He poured healing oil over her broken body. He held a cup to her lips and gave her bread to eat. A soft, white gown replaced her work-worn garments.

She had no words—only his name came to her lips. Over and over again she spoke it through the tears that washed her face.

Lifted to her feet, he led her to his throne. She saw intricately carved lettering arched across its high back forming the word GRACE—forgiving, cleansing, enabling grace. Grace to do what her King asked of her. Grace to finally rest at his feet and wait upon him.

"Task-oriented" is a term often used to describe people like me. If I have meaningful work and something to show for my efforts at the end of the day, I'm happy. I'm especially happy if the something I do results in helping others. But my natural bent is to focus on the task at hand, not necessarily to relate to the people I may be helping. It's the way a good many of us are wired, and I believe God puts us together that way for His purposes.

However, for much of my life I've succumbed to the great temptation to relate to God in a task-oriented manner. I want Him to give me a list of what needs to be done and let me get on with it. It's been a long, slow process, but He has taught me that although He has plans for my life and tasks for me to accomplish, He is a very relational being and wants *me* more than He wants what I may do for Him. In fact, I've discovered the hard way that if I put the task before my relationship with Him, I eventually become worn out and joyless—also according to His plan. He won't share His place in my heart with anyone or anything.

Listen to God's heart for us in this paraphrase of Matthew 11:28–30:

> Are you tired? Worn out? Burned out on religion? Come to me. Get away with me and you'll recover your life. I'll show you how to take a real rest. Walk with me and work with me—watch how I do it. Learn the unforced rhythms of grace. I won't lay anything heavy or ill-fitting on you. Keep company with me and you'll learn to live freely and lightly (MSG).

What a marvelous God we have! He wants us to live life *with* Him, not just *for* Him. And as a by-product of living life *with* Him, we get to participate in His purposes that grow out of the life and love we share. Or, as John 15:5 says, we bear fruit as a result of abiding in Him and letting Him abide in us.

First of All a Daughter

Lord, I know You want me to spend time with You, but I feel guilty when I'm not busy.

Daughter, our love for one another is foundational to every other area of your life. This is not a step to something else. Relationship is the foundation upon which everything else is built and which continues to hold it all up. Neglect relationship, and nothing can stand up under time and pressure.

But so much needs to be done.

Yes, but in My way and in My time. Too much busyness will distract and hinder you from following My plans for you. Even your desire to serve can take My place in your heart. You are not primarily a servant—you are first of all My daughter.

Forgive me, Lord, but I think I'm more comfortable with the idea of serving You than being close to You.

You are forgiven, daughter, and greatly loved. I am pleased with you and am teaching you My ways. But I am a Person, and I want you to know Me as a Person. I am not a project to be mastered or accomplished. In order to serve Me well, you must know Me well. Give yourself to worship. Learn of Me. Rekindle your devotion.

Please change me, Lord, so that I can be what You want me to be.

Beloved, I love you as you are. My love won't grow stronger as you "get better." You are My precious child, and nothing will make Me love you more than I do right now. But I am working to perfect My love in you. "… perfect love drives out fear" (1 John 4:18).

Whom Do You Serve?

Our time together is wonderful, Lord, but when do I get to *do* something?

Can I do with you as I want, beloved? If I ask you to just wait upon Me, will you do it? Lay down your desire to be used. Quiet your soul, and wait upon Me.

Whom do you serve, daughter?

I serve You, Lord.

Then let Me have responsibility for showing you how to serve Me. I will not let you miss My will.

The Goal Is . . .?

Lord, I feel driven to keep serving You, but I feel I've lost my way and the purpose of it all.

Satisfy the heart of God. Make that your goal. Don't let needs drive you; let love for Me compel you. I invite you to join Me in My heart's pursuits. Like the child in Psalm 131, I invite you to look out with Me at the needs around you. I see things differently than you do, and I will give you a new perspective. I am the Creator, and I never lack creative resources to meet the needs I see.

Fruit-Bearing

Lord, I see the barren tree You are showing me. That is how I feel—barren. What do You want me to understand from it?

In the winter the tree is dormant and stores up strength and nourishment for the spring so it can bloom and produce fruit. The tree must endure the harsher conditions of winter to grow strong. I don't look for the same kind of fruit in the winter season as I do in the spring and summer. But the tree is still alive and well, and hidden things are happening in which I take just as much pleasure.

You are in a winter season, daughter. You see little outward fruit, but as you put your roots down deeper into Me and My love for you, you are becoming stronger for the fruitful time ahead. Don't be anxious and impatient for the fruit-bearing season: everything in its own time.

I love you and delight in you in every season. Live fully in this present season.

"I Can't...I'm Not...I'm Too..."

Lord, I'm hearing the words: "I can't...I'm not...I'm too..." This *is* how I feel so much of the time when I think of serving You. What are You saying to me, Lord?

Daughter, I want no more excuses for lack of faith. No more excuses for pride and fear. Hear Me, beloved. What you are, I know. What you aren't, I know. Neither impresses Me nor hinders Me. What you are is Mine. You are sealed with My Spirit. You have My stamp of approval on you. Wear it with confidence and dignity. Am I enough, or not? Am I able to do what I have said I will do, or not?

You are able, Lord. You are enough.

Good. Now let's live this day together.

Poured Out

Lord, *dying to self* and *giving my life away* require vulnerability. I'm not comfortable with the exposure to others You are asking of me.

Beloved, you need people and they need you. You must refuse to let fear make you a prisoner. I want to give you away as a blessing to others. Let Me pour you out on the lives of others. There is great joy awaiting you as you give yourself away.

Keep stretching out, daughter. Push out your self-imposed barriers of limitation, and you will discover that I am big enough to meet you there in whatever your need may be. It pleases Me when you put My love and words to the test. Come, daughter, and live the life I have given you fully. Keep stepping away from fear and venturing out in faith.

Love is an act of giving—always giving away. Give yourself away—your time, your energy. It is in giving that you will receive all you need to keep giving. I'm a generous God. Put Me to the test. See if you can out-give Me. Join Me in the joy and adventure of giving your life away.

Lord, Your joy and enthusiasm for life take my breath away! I feel like such a dull plodder. I want very much to venture out with You into life more and more. Help me to obey You. Drag me along with You when I get stubborn or start to close in on myself. I know You want my eager, willing obedience, but my own nature is a strong force to be reckoned with, and I need Your powerful tug to break me loose from old patterns and fears. So drag me along if need be, dear Lord and Friend, until I fall into step with You more naturally. I want to be "poured out," but no one knows this bottle better than You.

Your obedience thus far is a delight to Me, daughter. There's much more sparkle in the bottle than you know.

On the Shelf?

I was struggling with feelings of having been set aside from a ministry I had been involved with, so I asked the Lord about it. In answer to my questions, the Lord gave me a simple picture of a pitcher filled with water. Then He said:

Pitchers don't pour themselves out, daughter. They hold the water and stay available and ready for the master's use. Die to self-motivated desire to be useful. Stay clean and available, but leave to Me the responsibility for pouring you out.

What's driving you to do more is not My Spirit, beloved. Dissatisfaction does not come from Me. A pitcher rests until it is picked up by the master. Be content to wait and rest, and trust Me not to forget you. You are becoming a vessel fit for noble purposes, but you must be patient (2 Timothy 2:20–21). We are cleaning the vessel so it can hold pure, clean water. That is what you want, isn't it?

Yes, Lord. You know my heart better than I do.

Good. If that's what you want and that's what I want, then it's as good as done! Now leave the process to Me. I know how to clean My vessels, and I know the purpose for which I created them.

Comparison

Lord, others do so much more than I seem able to do.

Beloved, I have called you to Myself, not to a task. Others get this out of order as well, so don't follow others, follow Me. What have I asked you to do? Don't worry and fret about what others are doing. Staying close to Me is your task.

My plans for you do not change, daughter. Your disappointment in yourself makes you fear that your life will have no value. I am not a harsh taskmaster. I don't love you one minute and reject you the next because of your performance. My love is pure, complete in itself, and eternal. You need only receive it, not earn it.

I'm delighted that you want to serve Me, but I don't love you more or less because of your success in doing that. Let Me be the judge of your effectiveness. I am your teacher, and only I give the grades. I don't evaluate you by comparing you with others. I am the Lord. Everyone answers to Me, not to one another.

Cart Before the Horse

In a time of feeling overwhelmed by worries and responsibilities following my father's debilitating stroke, the Lord gave me two contrasting pictures that made me laugh at myself while learning a very important lesson that would help carry me through the chaotic days that followed.

The first picture was of a little horse behind a heavily loaded cart. It was trying to push the cart uphill with its head while a cruel taskmaster beat the horse, demanding that it do the impossible.

The second picture showed the little horse hitched correctly to the front of a reasonably loaded cart and being lovingly led along by its master. As they moved along the path, the master would load and unload the cart with just the right weight for the little horse to carry.

Occasionally the master would stop to provide food and drink and rest, according to the horse's need.

What a revealing picture of my trying to "get the job done" in my own strength! Take the lead once again, Master!

The Big Picture

Sometimes my desire and efforts to be a "good Christian" are self-serving and hinder me from seeing and entering into the much bigger picture of what God is doing in the world around me. I can be fooled into thinking that I'm being spiritual, when actually, self is still in center ring trying to get its needs met.

The question came to me one day: What's worth dying for? As I thought about it, I saw two contrasting pictures. The first picture was of a small house. There was a person inside the house who completely filled it. I realized this was a picture of self and self's little world.

The next picture was huge. A gloriously bright sun filled the left side of the picture, and its light spread out in front of it. The right side of the picture was very dark, and there were millions of shadowy, human forms in the darkness. In the center of the picture, a very tiny person walked forward in the light of the sun toward the darkness. A cross moved in front of the person as they walked forward.

I realized this was a picture of God's kingdom advancing as each of us follows Jesus in whatever He asks us to do. Though we are small when compared to the Big Picture of what God is doing in the world, our part is important. When combined with the obedience of our brothers and sisters, our obedience to God will result in His kingdom advancing and the darkness losing its hold on captive people.

God showed me through this visual that I have choices to make every day concerning whether to let self rule my life, or to join Him in His work of carrying light and life to others who are held captive in some way by the darkness.

I'm amazed that He can use me in the Big Picture—that it matters one way or another if I do my part. It seems so small. But He says it matters—He says that following Him is even worth dying for.

ENTER IN ...

Lord, thank You for calling me daughter rather than servant. I know I am both, but being called daughter reminds me that You are my Father and not my employer. It also reminds me that it is family business we are doing and that love for Your children is what motivates You.

Thank You for loving me to Yourself, Father, when I was so lost. Please use me however You will in the family business of bringing sons and daughters home to You.

Your beloved

CHAPTER 8

God of the Here and Now

GOD ISN'T IN a hurry. But it seems everyone else is. The pressure to keep up can put us on a fast track that leaves us anxious and breathless at the end of the day. I find I can get so caught up in the swirl and rush that I neglect living in the *now* in my frenzy to prepare for tomorrow.

Perhaps like me, you catch your breath every now and then and ask yourself, "Is this really the way God intends for me to live? Am I doing it right?"

Though hard to practice in our fast-paced, produce-or-get-out-of-the-way culture, I believe our God of the Here and Now does have a better way for us to live our busy lives.

Live in the NOW

Lord, there is so much to do in this hurting world, and yet You seem unhurried, as if we had unlimited time to spend talking together.

It gives Me great joy to spend time with My children. I answer to no man's clock. Time is a measure for you, not for Me. I am not rushing to meet a deadline, daughter; I am the Lord. I am not bound by anyone's timetable.

I live in the eternal NOW, and I invite you to share "now" with Me. I want you to learn to be very present in the now. What am I saying to you? What are you seeing? What have I given you to do now?

I will be with you in the future, even as I am with you in the present. You can leave the future to Me. Don't worry about finding My will for the future—find Me and you find My will. As you live in Me and we share life together, you live in My will.

Receive My peace, daughter, and live in the present with Me. I will never love you more than I do right now. You will never be more useful to Me than you are right now. You will gain new abilities and skills perhaps, but you can be 100% in My will this present moment. This is abundant life, beloved. Today, here, now, be Mine and draw close. That is all I ask of you.

Rest? With So Much To Do?

Daughter, let it all go—all the striving and cares. Let Me carry them, and find rest for your soul.

I want to obey You in this, Lord, but I don't know how. I have responsibilities, and others depend on me to keep life running smoothly. I have concerns that cause anxiety. How do I rest and still keep up with all that I need to do?

Walk with Me in this day. Share with Me the concerns of this day. Remember, beloved, we are living life together. The burdens are lighter when they are shared. Life will never be burden-free, but burdens shared with Me won't overwhelm you. Be anxious for nothing; trust Me for everything. Learn the way of faith for the needs of this day.

My Need for You Is So Selfish

Lord, I realize that all too often I'm not seeking You for Yourself alone, but for comfort or help or power. How can I be changed to want just You and not what You do for me?

You need Me for all of that which you just mentioned. I want you to ask Me for all that you need. Ask more of Me. I am a good and generous Father, and I take great delight in providing for My children. As You see My provision in answer to prayer, you come to know and love Me more. Don't feel guilty for needing Me. I have created you to find all that you need in Me.

Who's in Control?

Lord, do I have the right balance in my life?

Balance is not as important an issue as you suppose, daughter. What matters is hearing and obeying Me. Only I know the proper balance for your life. Balance is sometimes just human control. Do you want human order and control, or do you want My order and control in your life? They are very different and produce very different results. Let Me order your days for you.

I am teaching you to walk in the Spirit with Me. That is the way to fullness and abundance of life. Let go of the controls and desire for balance, and let Me set the pace for your days. Yield your life fully to Me and see what I am able to do.

Spiritual Circulatory System

Beloved, life isn't found in external things, but in the deep wells of refreshing you will find only in Me. I know you know this, but you must believe it at a deeper level so the very fabric of your life is dependent on your experience of Me and My love for you. Life flows from the inside out, not the outside in.

How, Lord?

Time in My presence is your food and drink. You must make time for this, for I am your life. Be greedy for more of Me. Only I can satisfy the hunger of your soul. Hear Me, beloved, I am your life—your spiritual blood. Just as your physical being is dependent on blood being carried to every part, so your non-physical being is dependent on My life being carried to every part. My Spirit and your spirit must be in constant communion or death begins to set in.

Keep your spiritual circulatory system healthy, and life will be the result.

Ordinary, Everyday Life

Beloved, do you have time for Me?

Yes, Lord. Thank You for stopping me from rushing off to get things done without visiting with You. You know how anxious I get when I have several matters that need my attention.

I stopped you because you need Me, daughter. Refresh yourself in My love for you. Let this be a day of creative activity together. The things you must do will never satisfy you unless they are shared with Me.

Lord, my "to do" list is made up of everyday responsibilities. Are these the kinds of things You want to share with me? They seem so ordinary and unimportant compared with the serious needs in our world.

Daughter, most of human life is made up of the ordinary. If you only allow Me to meet with you in the extraordinary matters, not much is left for us to share! I delight in living your ordinary life with you. In fact, it is only in living the ordinary with Me that you will be able to enter into the extraordinary.

The routine matters of your day take on new purpose when you share them with Me. I say this to encourage you to persevere. Seek Me in your day-to-day, moment-by-moment life. Talk with Me, laugh with Me, listen to Me. Become familiar with My voice and My ways. In doing so, you will bring both of us great pleasure as we share life together.

The things I have called you to do are all around you each day. Be faithful in those things and let Me have the responsibility for whatever comes next.

Beloved, the important thing to learn is to follow My lead. I don't want to be structured into your day; I want to be your day—all of your life shared with Me, the Lord of Life. This is not an impossible goal. This is My will for you. We will not give up on this goal, because the rewards will be great.

God Sets the Pace

Lord, am I keeping in step with You?

Beloved, we will walk together for all eternity. I am not in a rush, and I will not rush you. My love is patient. Be patient with yourself and with Me. You don't realize how far you have come already. The journey is long and requires many faithful, single steps to accomplish it. And it is those faithful steps I see and take delight in. Won't you hold My hand and enjoy the journey with Me? I know where we are going, and I am able to get you there. Trust Me and be at peace.

I Think I'm Catching On!

I'm to live *with* Jesus, not just *for* Him. There's a big difference. One is based on relationship, the other on doing things. He wants people He can relate to, not driven, impersonal servants who fear failure. He invites me to be His friend and confidante. To live with Him as His early disciples did.

I want this way, Lord.

I want this way, too. You were created for this—to share life with Me.

Is it possible this side of heaven, Lord? For me?

It is possible and necessary. Life will crush you with loneliness, otherwise.

Is This Really You?

In a time of quiet, I had a picture of Jesus and myself riding horses—very fast! He was laughing and obviously enjoying the experience. He looked so human, and His capacity to enjoy and experience life was breathtaking—I can hardly describe it.

Then we got off the horses and sat on the edge of a high cliff, dangling our legs. I could see an eagle flying over the trees in the valley far below.

As I said, "This can't be what You're really like, Jesus—not so human and down to earth," I thought I heard Him say, *Why do you think My disciples had such a hard time believing in Me? I lived a very human life, with My feet always touching the ground. Your inclination, as was theirs, is to push Me away—to separate Me from the everyday human experience. But I am the God who is among you, the God of the here and now, the God who loves life and loves relationship. Please don't relegate Me to just the holy and mystical. Let's live life together. I have infinite capacity for all of life, and I will increase your capacity for life if you will let Me. Let go of your fears and hang on to Me—for dear life!*

ENTER IN …

If you haven't already done so, you may enjoy reading a well-known little book entitled *The Practice of the Presence of God* by Brother Lawrence.

Although he lived in the seventeenth century, Brother Lawrence has inspired countless Christians right up to the present day, and he is an excellent example of someone who learned to live with God in his moment-by-moment, everyday life.

CHAPTER 9

Through the Valley

～✤～

LOVE LED HER to the edge of a deep valley and, pointing down into the valley, said, "This is the way."

She looked over the edge and saw a rough, narrow path descending into the murky gloom. "Lord, this can't be your way for me! Surely there is a higher, lighter path that I can follow."

With Love's kind yet determined look, and still pointing into the valley, he replied, "Resurrection follows death."

She began her descent, questioning each painful step of loss. Familiar sights, familiar faces, were soon blotted out by the darkness covering her path. She stumbled many times as she felt her way along—perplexed and grieving.

Just enough light to keep her on the path filtered through her gloomy descent. The burden of loss grew heavier with each step, but so did her confidence that this was, indeed, the way chosen for her.

As she approached the deepest place in the valley—her burden heavy and overwhelming—she heard the sound of running water. She continued cautiously down the dark, narrow path.

Suddenly, light broke through the darkness to reveal a stream flowing beside the path. Love himself stood there waiting for her. His smile was radiant! Catching her hands up in his, he led her into the *stream and began twirling her around, splashing and dancing in the water. Love's infectious joy flooded her as she danced with him.*

Refreshed now and rested, her burden much lighter, she dared at last to ask, "Is this the end of my journey through the valley, Lord?"

Gazing deeply into her soul, he smiled the most tender of smiles and, pointing to the path ahead, answered, "Beloved, resurrection follows death."

Her burden now bearable, she started on her way again, certain that Love himself would continue to surprise her with joy when she least expected it.

Loss. Death. Not my favorite memories and experiences, but inevitable this side of heaven. Perhaps, like me, you've discovered that death has many faces.

Death of loved ones is certainly one of the hardest losses we can experience. Within seven years, my entire family of birth died—first my mother, then my father, then my much-loved brother. Perhaps someone who reads this will have suffered the even more devastating loss of children or a spouse. A close friend of mine lost two young daughters in one day as they crossed the street on their way to school. How does a person recover from such a tragedy? And yet her daily walk with God and trust in God testify to His ability to do the impossible and bring life out of death.

Sometimes we experience loss and suffering at the hands of others who sin against us out of their own brokenness. To live free of the pain, grief, and anger this can produce in us, we must keep our hand in the Lord's and let Him show us the way through the loss to forgiveness. It can be a long, difficult road. Each of us, if we've lived long enough, has a story to tell in this regard.

There is also a sense of death and loss when we must give up certain expectations of how life or people should treat us. It may be related to a broken or difficult marriage, relationships with children, unmet career goals, or dreams set aside because of illness.

And then there is the death that is perhaps the hardest of all and requires the greatest struggle: death to our self. I like the way the Amplified Bible describes it in Luke 9:23:

> And He said to all, If any person wills to come after Me, let him deny himself [disown himself, forget, lose sight of himself and his own interests, refuse and give up himself] and take up his cross daily and follow Me [cleave steadfastly to Me, conform wholly to My example in living and, if need be, in dying also].

Yes, death comes in many forms, and if it weren't for our Redeemer God who delights in turning broken glass into precious gems, life would be a pretty sorry business. But "resurrection follows death," and letting God walk us through our suffering always leads to new or renewed life. He will never abandon us in the valleys. In fact, it seems the deepest valleys can lead to our deepest experiences of true, God-given joy.

The Valley of the Shadow

The story related at the beginning of this chapter comes from an encounter I had with the Lord when I asked Him for a special time just to be with Him. Immediately, I saw us in a deep, narrow valley on the edge of a little river. The Lord held my hands and led me into the water where we danced and splashed like children. It was such a joyful, carefree time that I wondered how such delight and childlike play could possibly be right in a world of such great suffering. I was having a hard time reconciling this revelation of a joyful Jesus with the Jesus I knew who carried the grief and sorrow of the world. I could not understand how joy and suffering could be experienced at the same time.

I prayed: Lord, I feel You touching dry, brittle places in my soul and pouring in clean, sparkling water. You are captivating! Surprising! You are breaking all the sides out of the box I keep putting You in.

I believe I just heard You say that this is the Valley of the Shadow of Death. Again, You are turning my human understanding inside out and upside down. Thank You for this flood of joy and light into an area of tremendous potential darkness. Can it be that this river of refreshing, this joyous place of meeting, is right in the deepest part of that Valley?

Thank You, Lord, for bringing me here. I don't know why You have shown me this right now, but please help me to remember the feelings of these moments if and when I am drawn into the Valley.

Two weeks after this meeting with the Lord, my father had a stroke that led to his death one month later. My brother also died within the next two years of cancer. This vision from the Valley has encouraged and comforted me many times in the painful loss of my family.

Dying to Self

As I mentioned earlier, my greatest struggle with death has been willingness to die to self and my own self-protective ways. What I am learning in the ongoing struggle is that I have to let go of the false security of the known and familiar in order to experience the life God invites me to share with Him. It's a way of life that began by faith and now must be lived out by faith, moment-by-moment, as I make choices to die to myself and simply trust God.

The Lord used a picture to expose my self-protective ways. I saw myself holding my nose with one hand. My other hand was stretched up in the air, just as a child would do before jumping into a swimming pool. Then I was immersed in a large body of water.

This is what I understood from the picture:

The large body of water represented life in Christ, and it was the Lord's desire to immerse me completely into His life. He wanted me to breathe Him in deeply, to live more fully in the atmosphere of His presence: inhaling and exhaling Christ. But I was holding my nose, or trying to "save my life" as the Bible puts it (Luke 9:24).

I see what I have been doing, Lord. I've been hanging on to my life and my right to independence and control, rather than yielding control to You. It's frightening, Lord, to let go and lose my life in Your life: to let go of my nose, so to speak.

Please forgive me for holding my breath spiritually, Lord. Take away my fear and help me to give my life away to You completely.

Beloved, by losing your life for My sake, you lose nothing and gain everything (See Luke 9:23–26).

Into the Desert

During a certain season of my life, it seemed that everything I depended on to feel good about myself was being stripped away: the ministry I was involved in, the people I had been close to, even the sense of God's presence and approval. My knee-jerk response to this stripping was to look for ways to cover the areas of my life that had been left empty and exposed. I progressed through a range of emotions. The first was sheer terror at feeling naked and abandoned. Who was I, and where did I belong? The next was desperation to cover myself by finding new ways to prove my life had meaning. When my attempts to replace what I had lost failed, fear set in that perhaps neither God nor man had use for me. This was eventually followed by resignation to the fact that I could not "fix" this situation; God Himself seemed to be blocking my every effort. At last, by God's grace, I experienced peace when I was finally willing to trust His good intentions toward me and wait upon Him.

Though it took a while, I began to see God's hand in the losses I had experienced, and to understand why He had allowed them. Slowly, I realized that by taking away my props, God had exposed a needy, striving person who did not know how much I was loved or that God's love was a love I could fully rest in. During this silent, desert time, God began to turn my focus from my imperfect self to His perfect love that could heal my brokenness and fill the empty places in my soul.

He told her to wait—to just wait here in the desert.

Feeling somewhat peeved, she questioned again why he hadn't left her in the meadow they had passed through. It was lovely—so cool and green. And peaceful? It seemed nothing could trouble her there. And he always felt nearby when she needed someone to talk to.

But here? It was dry and barren, and silent as the grave. And though he promised he would never leave her, she had never felt so alone.

"Maybe he has finally decided I'm not worth his effort," she thought. "And I wouldn't blame him for that. Keeping company with just myself these days has been very eye opening. Now I'm left to wonder why he invited me along in the first place."

He had done an interesting thing right before he left her there. He put a small, wooden cross in her hand and said, "In this desert you will learn what it means to love and be loved."

She knew he wouldn't lie to her, but knowing herself as she did now, she felt less lovable than ever before.

But something very strange had begun to happen—so strange it was distracting her completely from her usual groveling in her inadequacies and failures. The small, wooden cross he had placed in her hand was growing! She watched amazed and full of wonder as it grew, and grew, and grew …

When aspects of my life that I felt most defined me as a person were taken away, I realized that I had nothing to offer God but my imperfect self. The unconditional, supernatural quality of His love for me began to stand out clearly for the first time, and I began to understand as never before what Paul meant when he said he boasted only in the cross (Galatians 6:14).

I learned two foundational lessons from this desert season. The first: *I am God's beloved.* Secure in His love, I don't *need* other people's approval, or a list of successes in life to prove my worth. Therefore, I am free to love and serve more unselfishly, for Jesus' sake rather than my own. The second: *I am the object of His mercy and grace.* I can do absolutely nothing to gain more favor with God than I already have by being *in Christ.* That is my identity. All else may change or be lost, but forever I will be His beloved, the object of His mercy and grace.

Once I began to rest in these truths, God led me out of the desert and into more life than I have ever known—life that grows out of the fertile ground of His love that is finally established in my heart. Another way of saying it might be, "resurrection follows death."

ENTER IN ...

I have told you these things, so that in me you may have peace. In this world you will have trouble. But take heart! I have overcome the world.

—John 16:33

One thing we can count on—we will spend part of our journey here on earth in the valley of loss.

But perhaps you've discovered as I have, that it is the people who have spent time with God in some of the deepest, darkest valleys whose lives are the most inspiring.

I may never have the courage (or foolishness) to ask God for valley experiences to grow me. But I hope that when they come, I will not respond to them with resentment or bitterness, but will let God produce in me what I have so admired in others.

CHAPTER 10

Battle Worn

—⦿—

THE BODY OF water spanned a great distance from shore to shore. The soldier standing by its edge strained to see the other side.

There was a definite droop to her head and shoulders. Even her armor couldn't hide the droop. And her eyes—oh, her eyes said it all: longing, fatigue. It was all there in her eyes.

From one hand hung a sword, as if she hadn't strength enough to return it to its scabbard. Anyone could see the sword was battle worn.

Though the soldier couldn't actually see the far shore, she had heard first-hand accounts of the other side, reports that painted glorious, vivid images in the mind's eye. Yes, she could see it all right. Sometimes the other side seemed more real than the ground she walked on.

The ground she walked on...

She could hear the battle raging behind her, just over the ridge, but she had no strength. She wasn't ready yet to go back.

What was it the Commander said about the other side? No enemies? Yes, that was it. Imagine that, no enemies. Sometimes she thought she was her own worst enemy. But the Commander said even that battle would end.

No sickness, death, tears; a new, strong body that would never grow old; adventures with him for ages without end; and, oh yes, a great feast with all those who follow him.

All of that waiting over there...

She hadn't sensed the Commander approaching until she felt a hand on her shoulder.

When she turned to face him, eager to apologize for leaving the battle, she was struck by the compassion in her Commander's eyes.

With his scarred, powerful hand on her shoulder, her Commander said, "I know you are weary. Receive my strength." The warrior felt herself being straightened, strengthened. Fresh courage, fresh resolve flowed into her.

"Now, come, follow me. The enemy holds many in his power that belong to me. We must free them and invite them to my feast."

Together they turned from the water's edge, and side-by-side walked back over the ridge to the battle.

We don't follow Jesus very long before we discover that we're in a battle. God has an enemy, Satan, who hurts Him by attacking those He loves. What better way to cause Him pain, as any parent can attest. We also have an enemy in ourselves that opposes God—our sinful nature. Then the human cultures in which we live pressure us to conform to ways that also stand in opposition to God. From within and without, we are continually challenged to go any way but God's. It can wear us down.

Life has taught me that when I choose to stay on the sidelines and disengage from the battle, I become spiritually dull and complacent. I end up giving the devil an easy target. So partly out of self-defense, I'm learning to use the weapons God has provided and stay close to Jesus. And, like it or not, staying close to Jesus means I find myself in the battle, because that's where He is.

As I understand it, the battle is all about people, like you and me. God is rescuing us from the darkness that opposes Him in our lives and then planting us firmly in His kingdom of light. Because God's heart is a Father's heart, He invites us to join Him in this search and rescue work, until every one of His children is safely home and embracing the life He offers them.

How we are used in the battle is up to our Commander and is as unique as we are.

The Cost of Intimacy

What will You hold me accountable for when I stand before You, Lord? What should I be doing when You return?

Listening to Me and obeying what you hear is My will for you, daughter. If I were to give you a list of assignments, you would set about getting the job done as best you knew how. In focusing on the task you would neglect Me, the source of your joy and power. Powerless and joyless, you would soon grow discouraged and lose your way back to Me.

My will must be done in My way. My way for you is by My side, listening to My voice, sharing life together, delighting in one another's company. Will you be a sharer of the way with Me?

Beloved, think of it this way: "The Lord and I will live this day together." I will be with you as you work and serve and love those around you. I will give you grace to do these things joyfully. As you go about your day, faithful in the tasks before you, I will draw you into My heart to share the concerns that are there. We will become intimates, sharing life together—nothing too small to be significant to the other. You will develop a listening ear to hear My instructions and counsel.

Trust Me, and I will use your life; I will not waste it. But your usefulness will only come out of a trusting relationship with Me—never apart from relationship.

Walk quietly with Me and aspire only to Me. Let Me be your ambition, your goal, your fulfillment. I have called you to Myself, not to a task.

Lord, I keep asking You for something important to do for You, and You keep giving me Yourself. Thank You for Your patience with my slowness to learn.

Daughter, your tendency is to sentimentalize what I have just said to you—to undervalue relationship. I have not called you to ease and comfort. I have called you to My side. Look at My side. What do you see?

A spear mark, Lord.

Yes, it is costly to walk beside Me. What is aimed at Me will sometimes hit you. Never forget that when suffering comes. I have not invited you for a quiet stroll through daisies. I lead a mighty army—but an army of lovers. My intimates are my co-laborers.

Who Do You Think You Are?

A strong spiritual attack came against me one day. I heard: "Who are you to think you're special to God? Why would He take a personal interest in you? Fool! Who do you think you are?"

"Lord, this voice is drowning out Your voice, and I'm having a hard time remembering what You have said to me. Help me, Lord!"

Shortly after calling out to God, I felt faith and strength flow into me, and I was able to pray:

"Even if everything the enemy accused me of were true, my hope is in You, Lord. You are all that I am not. My hope and salvation are in You and You alone. You are worthy, You are lovely, You are kind and forgiving, You are all that is lovable! And You are mine! If in nothing else, I will rejoice in this fact that You have drawn me to Yourself and I am Yours. Yes, I am foolish at times. Yes, I disappoint myself and other people. Yes, sometimes I am far from lovable, but I belong to You, Jesus, and You delight in me! This is my joy, my reason for living, my claim to fame—Jesus in me! And You, Lord, are gracious enough, lovely enough, kind enough, good enough to cover all my failings.

"I rest my case and demand that these accusations stop now! I glory in Jesus my King and my Friend!"

My mouth will tell of your righteousness, of your salvation
all day long, though I know not its measure… I will proclaim
your righteousness, yours alone.

—Psalm 71:15–16

*Daughter, you are exercising your spiritual muscles as you fight your
enemies. You have found the only solid ground on which to fight: My
righteousness and your place in Me. Remember this in the days to come.
Your enemies will try to force you to fight on their ground and keep you
off-balance with their accusations. When they attack you in areas of your
weakness, refer them to Me and My righteousness. That is the only defense
you need. That is the place of victory.*

*These lessons are difficult and painful, but they are critical to your
well-being. If I don't seem as near to you these days, it is for your good and
growth, not because I love you less or am weary of you. My love is persistent,
patient, and persevering. More important than your comfort is your ability
to stand against your enemies; this can only be learned in battle. I must make
you strong, and I use your enemies to do so. They are tools in My hand, and
therefore, you need not fear them.*

*You don't suffer these attacks because you are far from Me, but because
you are close. I am teaching you My ways, as you have asked. Be comforted
now and enter into My rest.*

"Baa"

When it is necessary to stand against the devil and his works, I am
sometimes so aware of his strength and my comparative weakness that
I become fearful. The Lord gave me a little illustration one day to show
me what happens in the spiritual realm when by God's direction I am
asked to engage in spiritual battle.

He showed me a roaring lion attacking a little sheep. The sheep
turned toward the lion and "baaed," as sheep do. Ordinarily, a sheep's
"baa" would have no effect on a lion, and the sheep would be quickly
devoured. But because the sheep was acting in obedience to the Great
Shepherd, and therefore had His authority and power backing it up,
instead of hearing the sheep's weak little "baa," the lion heard the mighty
roar of the Lion of Judah!

The Lord will roar from Zion and thunder from Jerusalem.
—Joel 3:16

...the Lion of the tribe of Judah, the Root of David, has
triumphed.
—Revelation 5:5

The devil isn't afraid of us for a minute, but *Jesus in us* is another
matter altogether.

Dressed for Battle

Lord, why do I feel so beaten up these days?

*Never forget that your battle is with powers of darkness (Ephesians
6:10–18). You have no strength to match these powers other than what I
give you. Your strength must come from Me. You must be prepared every
day for the battle. No soldier faces the enemy without careful preparation.
In your weariness you have grown careless. "Put on the full armor of God so
that you can take your stand against the devil's schemes" (Ephesians 6:11).
Don't discount this preparation out of familiarity with these verses. These
are life and instruction for you. Always prepare for battle.*

Strength in Numbers

One day I struggled with an attack of very negative thoughts. It felt
as though a dark cloud had settled on me. I decided to ignore it and
focus on praying for others. A wonderful time of intercession followed.
But then the oppression settled on me again so powerfully that my mind
was in a swirl of negative thoughts that bombarded me. The gist of it
was: "You're useless. Nobody cares about you. You're being overlooked
and neglected. God just humors you, but can't really use you. You'll
never change."

Because I had believed these lies most of my life, I was vulnerable
to them. The accusations had a ring of truth that made them hard to
resist. Even though I knew I shouldn't listen, my effort to silence the
lies wasn't working, and despair settled on me.

I decided to call a trusted friend and have her pray for me. She prayed that the accusations would dissipate and lose their hold on my mind. Within a very short time the oppression lifted, and I felt nothing of the despair and self-pity I had felt just a few moments before.

The important lesson I learned was that I need other Christians, and I must not let pride keep me from receiving the spiritual help of my brothers and sisters.

Help me remember, Lord, that I need others and they need me.

Standing Firm

So many reports say the darkness is closing in on Your people throughout the world, Lord. Are we losing the battle?

I see and understand men's plans and schemes, but I am in no way limited by them. Remember the Red Sea (Exodus 13:17–14:31). I know My purposes and the end of all things—that will never change. But men's choices are always theirs to make. Some are turning toward the Light, while others are being drawn deeper and deeper into darkness.

Don't be surprised at what you face these days. Be ready to suffer for My sake. You are inheriting an eternal Kingdom.

Stay vigilant and in My presence. I know My way for you. I will guide you. I will steady you. I will shield you by My power. But you must stay close. Choices matter a great deal.

All that you need, I am. Don't fear the future, for My hand is upon you to keep, protect, and sustain you in every circumstance.

Eyes on eternity

Because we live in the midst of a spiritual battle going on all around us and sometimes the darkness can seem overwhelming, the Lord reminded me how important it is to keep an eternal perspective on life. These verses have helped:

> For this world in its present form is passing away.
> —1 Corinthians 7:31b

Therefore keep watch, because you do not know on what day your Lord will come.

—Matthew 24:42

… prepare your minds for action; be self-controlled; set your hope fully on the grace to be given you when Jesus Christ is revealed.

—1 Peter 1:13

… if we endure, we will also reign with him.

—2 Timothy 2:12

May God himself, the God of peace, sanctify you through and through. May your whole spirit, soul and body be kept blameless at the coming of our Lord Jesus Christ. The one who calls you is faithful and he will do it.

—1 Thessalonians 5:23–24

The Lord will rescue me from every evil attack and will bring me safely to his heavenly kingdom. To him be glory for ever and ever.

—2 Timothy 4:18

Enter In ...

The reason the Son of God appeared was to destroy the devil's work.

—1 John 3:8

Much has been written in recent years about resisting and overcoming Satan and his works. Spiritual warfare is a reality of our Christian experience here on earth that should be given serious attention or we risk suffering the consequences.

Not knowing our enemy makes us vulnerable to his attacks. And not understanding the spiritual authority God has given us hinders our ability to partner with Jesus in seeing the devil's works destroyed and God's will accomplished.

Following are two excellent resources, which you may find helpful on the subject of spiritual battle. The first is a very readable and practical book by Dean Sherman entitled *Spiritual Warfare for Every Christian* (Seattle, WA: YWAM Publishing, 1995). The other is a chapter entitled "Authoritative Prayer" from a wonderful book by Richard Foster called, *Prayer: Finding the Heart's True Home* (New York, NY: HarperCollins Publishers, 1992).

CHAPTER 11

Restorer of My Soul

HOW AND WHEN God heals our soul's wounds depends primarily on His wisdom, power, and timing. However, I've learned that my *willingness* to let Him touch the painful places in my life is also a key to becoming whole. At times, healing requires the reopening of old wounds that continue to fester under scar tissue, and the process can be painful and disruptive to our lives. My tendency is to want to leave the past in the past, to just forgive and forget and get on with life. And that's what I tried to do for many years after becoming a Christian.

During those years, God blessed me with a wonderful husband, a precious daughter, good friends, meaningful work—so much to be grateful for. And yet, under the surface, I carried a weight of pain that only grew heavier as the years passed.

I will be eternally grateful to God that though I was willing to drag my broken parts along with me through life, He was not. He brought people of faith, prayer, and power into my life. Through them He revealed Himself to me as my wonderful counselor, my compassionate healer, my strong deliverer—the restorer of my soul. He started me on a journey of healing that continues to this day—a journey that has often required the opening of doors I once closed on the past.

An infant's wail caught her attention. Following the sound, she retraced her steps back down the long, gray corridor of unopened doors.

Yes, it was coming from behind that door.

Cautiously, she opened it and peered inside.

Immediately, the helpless wail of the infant and the cold sterile atmosphere of the room overcame her—entered her like a knife opening an old wound. She felt the sudden pain would swallow her whole.

As helpless now as the infant she had become, she stood rooted in place—time wrapping around itself to bring her back to this moment.

From behind her, a hand was placed on her shoulder and gently moved her aside from the doorway.

A man walked into the room where the baby lay crying. Picking the infant up into his arms, he motioned for her to follow him.

They passed through another door into a connecting room, warmed by soft morning sunlight coming through curtained windows. A woman sat in a rocking chair. Compassion shone on her gentle face as she reached for the baby with welcoming arms. Its pitiful cries were stilled as the man placed the infant in the woman's comforting embrace.

He turned then and looked into the eyes of his companion. As she held his gaze, the raw pain was drawn from her heart, and peace entered. The tears of her wailing became tears of cleansing—healing.

With another look at him and then at the infant—who was finally content in loving arms—she walked from the room, leaving the door open.

The gray corridor was a bit brighter now because of the soft light coming from the open door. She smiled a grateful smile as she started on her way again. The light would give her courage to face the unopened doors yet ahead of her, and she knew he would be there to walk with her through each one of them.

The little story related above is based on an experience I had of God opening a closed door in my heart. It falls into the "weird and wonderful" category of healing: *weird* because God exposed a wound of neglect that I had no way of actually remembering—though I lived with its effects, *wonderful* because I experienced healing as a result. Later in life, my mother, who was now a follower of Christ, and I were able to have candid talks that brought more healing to both our hearts.

I learned two important lessons from this experience. First, God is not limited to healing just the painful experiences we can actually remember. Second, God is my perfect Parent and is more than able to supplement any lack I experienced as a result of having imperfect human parents. *"Though my father and mother forsake me, the Lord will receive me"* is a promise from Psalm 27:10 that I have been reminded of many times. As a parent, I find comfort in applying this same truth to my own parenting failures.

God's healing work in my life has been at times instantaneous and other times painfully slow. It has been done in private and also in public. It has been both quiet and noisy, and, as mentioned above, it has at times seemed weird but the results always wonderful. He has used a wide variety of healing instruments to do His work: His written Word, people of prayer and wisdom, the counsel of His Spirit, dreams and visions, and my godly husband, who has loved me with an unconditional love throughout our many years together.

The restorer of our souls is unlimited in what He will use to cleanse, heal, and deliver His beloved from all that distorts His image in us.

Closed Doors

I had anxiety for so long that for me it was normal. It was all I knew. On rare occasions I would get a taste of peace and well-being, but they never lasted. These good feelings came and went so mysteriously that they seemed disconnected from any cause and effect pattern I could identify.

Then the Lord began to reveal to me that I was separating the real world of my life's experiences from my relationship with Him. I lived as if there were categories of life in which God was interested, and then there were others where I was on my own. Into this last group I put my inner struggles and unresolved hurts, as well as the everyday stresses of life. My feeling was that if I kept busy doing God's business, this would please Him, and my personal problems would take care of themselves in time.

But God had a different and better way, and He met with me in the throne room of my heart.

"Daughter... daughter."

She looked up from her prayers, and saw him looking at her with just the hint of a twinkle in his eye.

"Yes, Lord?"

"Do you hear something?"

"Uh, hear something, Lord?"

"Yes, I'm sure I hear knocking coming from behind those doors."

She glanced around the room at the many closed doors that lined the walls, and there was, indeed, a loud knocking coming from behind each one. The sound was a familiar one. It played the background to her busy days. It was annoying, of course, but could be ignored if she set her mind to it. It certainly wasn't anything the King should trouble himself about.

"Please answer the doors, daughter, and let's see what's banging on them."

Was he serious? Surely he didn't want those noisy intruders in this holy place with them—she knew she didn't. "Lord, I don't..."

But glancing at him, as she began to protest, she saw that he was very serious. She fell silent.

The noise from the doors grew louder by the minute—it was deafening in fact. However, even more alarming than the increased clamor was the effect it was having on her. Her heart raced, and her grown-up control was giving way to a child-like fear of the dark. Open those doors?

"Daughter, I am bigger and stronger than anything banging on the doors. We must open them and bring whatever is there into my presence and under my peace. Nothing must be left outside of our relationship to trouble and torment you."

"If you say so, Lord."

With a look at the King for reassurance, she walked to the first door, opened it, then ran back and clung to him. Whatever came through that door, they would face it together.

Opening closed doors and letting God walk me through them is an ongoing process. He will from time to time draw my attention to a noisy door He wants to open, and I'm surprised to find something behind the door that I thought I had already dealt with.

The issue of rejection, for example, has been one of those with many doors. As God began to heal and set me free from the spirit of rejection, He revealed to me how deeply rooted this enemy of my soul had become, and the many ways it manifested itself in my life. He led me through the process of forgiving those who had hurt me, repenting of sinful attitudes I had developed toward them and myself, exposing the lies I had believed, and laying hold of the truth of who I am in Christ.

My testimony is that God sets the captives free! But to stay free, I have to hang on to the truth and apply it every time I am tempted to fall back into old ways of thinking and acting. It is work.

One day the Lord brought to my mind a person I felt had rejected me. I had reverted to old patterns of negative thinking about myself, as well as critical thoughts of this person. The Lord broke into this old cycle and spoke to the very root of rejection in my life:

Daughter, you are deeply afraid that this person is right about your value or lack of value. But does it really matter what this person thinks? Does it make you a different person if people feel one way or another? Is your identity so fragile that I would let it be determined by people who don't know or love you as I do? Your identity is safe in Me. I am your life. No one can rob you of who I have created you to be, but yourself.

Beloved, I free you now of every judgment ever brought against you—real and imagined. You are cut off from them—separated from them by your death and resurrection with Me. Your life is hidden in Me. No one can rob you of who you are in Me. You share My life. Now, release this person from your need of this person's approval.

The Lord led me to cut my soul free from this person and others I had allowed to determine my worth. I saw myself bound to Jesus with cords of unfailing love—my identity and worth bound to Him alone.

Lord, forgive me for giving the power and responsibility to other people to determine my identity and value, rather than looking to You alone. You are the one who suffered and died to show how much You love and treasure me.

I give back to others the freedom to accept, be indifferent to, or reject me. That's their choice. With Your help I will do what I can to be a loving person and leave the results to You. When I sin against others, help me to see it, Holy Spirit, and then show me how to set things right. Please keep me growing in this area of loving and relating to people. I am Yours, and nothing of Yours is ever a lost cause. Thank You, wonderful Counselor!

Saying Good-Bye

Lord, I know You are calling me into a deeper place of fellowship with You, but I find myself drawing back. I'm afraid the closeness won't last. I also feel a strong need to protect myself from the vulnerability of too much closeness to anyone—even You. Being alone feels safer than exposing my need for love or acceptance.

After praying this, the Lord used a picture to begin the healing of my fear of closeness in relationships.

I saw myself as a young girl, peering into a dark, musty room through a partially open doorway. The room was filled with shadowy faces I couldn't distinguish but that I knew were people I had loved, moved away from, and never said goodbye to during my years growing up in a military family.

It was a sad, gloomy place, but the Lord wanted me to enter it. With Jesus' arm around me, we walked into the room. I began to weep the unshed tears of loss, and to grieve for the "deaths" of so many friends and family through separation as a child.

As the healing tears flowed, I thanked each one for loving me and giving my heart a place to belong for the short time I knew them. I told them I missed them. I said, "Goodbye. Go with God. Let Him love you as He has loved me, and take away your pain as He has mine."

The Lord brought light, hope, and joy into that room, and all the dark shadows left. I thanked Him for being a friend who has never left me and who never will.

One Piece at a Time

In a quiet moment with the Lord, He led me through a healing time of myself as a young girl. I saw a little girl sitting alone on the floor in a gray, colorless room, with small, broken pieces of things scattered all around her. She was looking at all the little broken things and feeling helpless, alone, and very sad.

I asked the Father to please touch the girl and heal her. From a deep place inside of me grief rose up. As I struggled with the surfacing pain, the Lord showed me Himself in the picture: I saw Him, in color, sitting next to the little girl, with the objects scattered around them both. He was warm and smiling and understood all the broken little pieces and what they meant.

Daughter, I am with you, and I know what to do. You don't have to fix yourself.

In response, I saw the little girl pick up one of the broken pieces, then turn and hand it to Jesus.

Lord, I see the truth You are showing me. I am not alone and helpless. I put my trust in You to take care of one broken piece of my life at a time. You are, and always have been, with me. You are my God, my healer.

The picture changed, and I saw the little girl, now in color, clinging to Jesus' neck just as tightly as she could, crying healing tears of joy. She knew she belonged to Him and always would. She knew He would never leave her alone. Finally she was safe and secure in His arms.

Lord, thank You for all the warmth and life and color You have given this picture. I receive by faith the healing of this little girl's broken parts and all she represents in me.

Safe in His Keeping

Like many people, I want to figure myself out—to understand the reasons why I feel a certain way, believing that will fix me. But the Lord made it clear through a picture that although He is the revealer of hidden things, some mysteries about my life will remain, and are safe in His keeping.

One morning I awoke and saw a picture of a pie with a piece missing. Jesus had the piece in His hand and let me know that it was safe with Him. He said that any parts of me that feel incomplete and clouded with unknowns, He will fill with Himself. My wholeness will result from being filled more with Jesus, not with being able to understand the missing pieces. He is my sufficiency. He is the One who satisfies my needs and completes me. The question marks are safe in His keeping.

A House Set in Order

One morning, as I met with the Lord, I saw a picture of a house leaning to one side. The house was badly in need of repair, but around the house was a well-maintained fence protecting it. This was what I heard Him say:

You have been content with mended fences, but I am repairing broken walls and foundations.

Lord, to be honest, I'm surprised You still see so much brokenness in me. I've been feeling much stronger these days, almost like the real me is finally able to stand up and get on with life and service. It's unsettling to think so much foundation and wall repairing still needs to be done.

Beloved, you are feeling the effects of the restoring work I have been doing. But I am letting you know that there is more to be done. Don't settle for less than My finished work, for your own sake as well as that of others. To the extent you short-circuit My repair work in you, you hinder what I can do through you.

You have asked Me to search your heart and go deep in uprooting all that hinders the flow of My Spirit in you. Remember this when you feel unsettled and uncomfortable. I can't leave everything in place and still do a thorough housecleaning. It will look and feel like upheaval and disorganization, but if you will trust Me for the outcome, then you will have grace for the process. You will have peace in chaos, confidence in turmoil, and strength in weakness.

I'm the Architect, daughter. I see the original plans. If you will give Me a free hand in the restoration process, the results will be a strong, sturdy house filled with light.

Fearfully and Wonderfully Made

My husband prayed for me one morning, but he kept referring to me by my maiden name. I finally asked him if he knew he had been using that name. He was surprised that he had, and said he hadn't thought of my maiden name for years.

We both sensed that it was the Holy Spirit prompting him to pray in this way, and that it was the young, unmarried me who needed to be prayed for. So he continued to pray, and as he did, the Lord began to reveal to me that when I married my husband I shut out my old identity with its sad, negative associations, and fully adopted a new identity as Pam Marhad. I began to see that the old me had never caught up, had never fully come into a love-grace-mercy relationship with Jesus.

Lord, thank You for showing me this. I come to You now to be joined to You more completely. I give You *all* of me. Lord, I want this part of me to be brought into the love relationship we share. I've ignored, disowned, and pushed her away all these years, but she's me, and You love her, so I must love her, too.

I feel strange praying this way, Lord. But I know You are doing a work in me that is deep and foundational. So whether I fully understand it or not, I trust You. Please bind all of me to You with strong cords of love, and let no part be left outside of Your love and grace. I want all of me joined to You in the deepest core of my being.

Happy day! More of me in love with Jesus!

Because this experience fits into the "weird and wonderful" category I mentioned earlier, I was very tempted to leave it hidden in my journal. But I can trace major breakthroughs in my life to the morning when my husband prayed for me by my maiden name. From that day I knew, as never before, that I was God's beloved, and the depression, rejection, and insecurity I had struggled with most of my life began to lose their hold on me.

Although this was a breakthrough moment, I know it was the culmination of years of God's healing of my soul. Through His Word, and through His faithful people, He had uprooted lies, planted truth, and loved me patiently, softening and readying my heart for this moment. The fruit of this experience has been an ability to love and relate to other people in a way I never thought would be possible.

We are *fearfully and wonderfully made* as the psalmist puts it in Psalm 139:14, complex and intricate by God's design. And in His wisdom, power, and perfect timing, God does the complex, intricate work of restoring our wounded souls to wholeness when life scatters us along the way. Praise His name!

ENTER IN ...

The Lord is close to the brokenhearted and saves those who are crushed in spirit.

—Psalm 34:18

No matter how scattered and broken some of us may view ourselves, we can rest in the confidence that God is much more concerned about our healing than we are. But the difference between Him and us is that He's not overwhelmed by our need or anxiously wringing His hands, wondering what to do about us. He has a plan. He knows what to do.

One of the names by which God has revealed Himself to us in Scripture is "The Lord Who Heals" (*Yahweh Rophe.* See Exodus 15:26). By this name He wants us to know that being a healer is part of His nature. It's who He is and therefore what He does.

If you haven't already done so, won't you invite The Lord Your Healer into your need? He may surprise you with His methods and confound you with His timing, but one day you will look back and say with David, "O Lord my God, I called to you for help and you healed me" (Psalm 30:2).

CHAPTER 12

Into His Presence

HE INTERRUPTED HER right in the middle of her telling him about her failures and the matters that made her so anxious these days.

His whispered words had a haunting, musical quality to them: "Beloved, come up a little higher... beloved, come up a little higher."

"But my concerns have weighed me down, and I don't know how to obey you."

"Step away, beloved, and come with me. My presence is what you need."

The strong, sweet invitation pulled her irresistibly to her feet and along the path before her. She followed his voice to the base of a gently flowing waterfall, where the path ended. Rocky, rough-hewn stairs led up the left side of the cascading stream. She began her ascent.

The way, though not treacherous, became steep enough that she was very grateful to see the one whose voice she followed reach out his hand to draw her up behind him. His look filled her with anticipation. His eagerness to surprise her with something wonderful was written all over his smiling face.

How she loved this one who led her!

Higher and higher still they climbed beside the tumbling waters, until it seemed they would reach the very top of the world.

Nearing the summit, her companion indicated that she was to continue on alone. Filled with anticipation, she climbed the remaining distance. She stepped up from the last rocky stair onto a smooth stone plateau, and her breath caught in wonder. All was still as she stood taking in the scene before her.

Stretching from horizon to horizon, the sky formed a blue-domed cathedral overhead. Through its soft hue shone the warming sun. An ageless stream, flowing from a distant, unseen source had worn a path into the stone plateau. It shimmered in the sunlight as it wove its way toward her.

Never had she imagined such a place could exist. And never had she been so completely alone—alone, yet not lonely. Life pulsed from every atom of the stark, beautiful landscape before her.

To her right lay a clear pool of water, a catch basin formed by the stream that flowed gently through it and then down the mountain. She didn't hesitate. She stepped into the sun-warmed water and lay back, letting its clean warmth envelope her. The anxious, troubling concerns she had brought with her were quickly carried away in its gentle flow. Her weariness, discouragement, and sense of failure washed away in the cleansing, life-giving waters, and peace took their place.

He had brought her to this wonderful place, surprising her with the power of his life soaking into her every pore. Saturated, immersed in his presence, she worshipped the one who had led her to this pool at the top of the world.

How much is set in order in my life, and my perspective is changed, when I respond to God's invitation to come away with Him to a quiet place and rest. It seems counter to reason to let it all go—all the matters clamoring for attention, the unsolved problems and the jumbled feelings—and just quietly to rest in God's presence. But the very thing my mind and flesh resist is God's solution to my anxious striving: stepping away from it all to be with Him.

One day, anxious and troubled about many things, I heard the whispered invitation related in the story above: "Come up a little higher.

Step away and come with Me. It's My presence you need." I wanted to respond to the Lord's invitation, but I didn't know how. In a beautiful visual aid, the Lord led me away from my anxious concerns to the waterfall and then the pool of refreshing. Jesus' presence was tangible, as was the peace that flooded me.

It wasn't a time for words. He had brought me there to just *be* in His presence. And though no word was spoken and no counsel given, my anxious heart was quieted and every concern put to rest by simply being with Him. Eventually I heard Him say:

Beloved, I have given you a picture of what it means to rest in My presence and be refreshed in My Spirit. It is a physical picture that speaks of a spiritual truth. I am that stream of water to you. I am the pool of cleansing, refreshing, and rest.

Slip away with me to this high and lovely place whenever you feel weighed down or weary. Here you will be washed and renewed. Here you will find strength for your days.

Since this experience, my best intention has been to regularly practice being quiet in God's presence—to learn to be still and know that He is God (Psalm 46:10). But I have come to realize that when the day's demands don't allow for extended time together, I can still go frequently to that pool of His presence. Just recalling the picture brings a deep sigh of relief and peace. He invites me to retreat with Him to that inner place of meeting often. There I am reminded that I am His beloved, and He alone is my life and strength.

ENTER IN ...

Let the following passages from God's Word wash over you as you sit quietly in His presence:

As the deer pants for streams of water, so my soul pants for you, O God. My soul thirsts for God, for the living God. When can I go and meet with God?

—Psalm 42:1–2

Continued....

Come, all you who are thirsty, come to the waters; and you who have no money, come, buy and eat! Come, buy wine and milk without money and without cost. Why spend money on what is not bread, and your labor on what does not satisfy? Listen, listen to me, and eat what is good, and your soul will delight in the richest of fare. Give ear and come to me; hear me, that your soul may live.

—Isaiah 55:1–3

I will sprinkle clean water on you, and you will be clean; I will cleanse you from all your impurities and from all your idols. I will give you a new heart and put a new spirit in you; I will remove from you your heart of stone and give you a heart of flesh.

—Ezekiel 36:25–26

… I provide water in the desert and streams in the wasteland, to give drink to my people, my chosen, the people I formed for myself that they may proclaim my praise.

—Isaiah 43:20–21

… whoever drinks the water I give him will never thirst. Indeed, the water I give him will become in him a spring of water welling up to eternal life.

—John 4:14

… I will make her deserts like Eden, her wastelands like the garden of the Lord. Joy and gladness will be found in her, thanksgiving and the sound of singing.

—Isaiah 51:3

Lord, You are my wonderful Shepherd. Thank You for leading me to quiet waters—for inviting me to come away with You and be refreshed in Your presence. You have restored my soul.

CHAPTER 13

Ever After

WE ARE GOD'S beloved. His arms are always open to welcome us. But we must know that responding to His invitation to draw near comes with a price. He will say to us: *Daughter, you have been satisfied with substitutes and fakes—imitations of real life. I intend to give you that which is authentic, pure, and priceless. But you must give to Me what you have clutched so tightly in your hands out of fear that there is nothing better for you.*

I know who I have created you to be, and the things you clutch have no place in the future I have planned for you. Give them to Me, and I will give you that which is real, beautiful, and eternal.

I know you, and I plan to remove all that hinders you from living the life for which you are destined. If you will take the daily steps of obedience I ask of you—steps that will lead you into an ever-deepening walk with Me—our joy will be full, and you will shine with the beauty of Jesus alive in you.

God's intentions for our lives are so much greater than anything we can imagine. As we cooperate with Him in the transformational work He wants to do in us, we *begin* the journey of living out our destiny. But our short life here on earth is just the beginning. It's just a foretaste of the fullness of His plans for us that will continue to unfold throughout endless ages.

"Dear friends, now we are children of God, and what we will be has not yet been made known" (1 John 3:2). This verse fills me with anticipation. As wonderful as it is to be His beloved here on earth, these words imply that what awaits us is even more inconceivably glorious than anything we have yet experienced or imagined.

Does it sound self-serving to think of our personal, eternal destinies? Yes, it does to me as well. But God must have a different perspective, because He is forever tantalizing us with words such as:

No eye has seen, no ear has heard, no mind has conceived what God has prepared for those who love him...
—1 Corinthians 2:9

I consider that our present sufferings are not worth comparing with the glory that will be revealed in us.
—Romans 8:18

For our light and momentary troubles are achieving for us an eternal glory that far outweighs them all.
—2 Corinthians 4:17

In his great mercy he has given us new birth ... into an inheritance that can never perish, spoil or fade—kept in heaven for you...
—1 Peter 1:3–4

... our citizenship is in heaven. And we eagerly await a Savior from there, the Lord Jesus Christ, who, by the power that enables him to bring everything under his control, will transform our lowly bodies so that they will be like his glorious body.
—Philippians 3:20–21

Then the righteous will shine like the sun in the kingdom of their Father.
—Matthew 13:43

My attitude toward passages like these that refer to our future glory in heaven has changed in recent years. Perhaps it's due in part to getting older, but I think it has more to do with a fresh realization that life is continuous from the moment of our conception through ages without end.

At some point, each of us who belongs to Christ will go through a split-second shift from earth to heaven—at last, face-to-face with Jesus. But we will continue to exist as ourselves, just as Jesus did after His death and resurrection. We are becoming *now*, by God's power and grace, what He will enhance and build upon throughout endless ages.

The effect this understanding of our Christian life has on me is three-fold:

1. I'm much more serious about using my comparatively few years on earth learning to delight in God and to serve in His Kingdom. I'd like to "hit the ground running," so to speak, when I get to heaven, and not have to spend the first few thousand years playing catch-up or getting over culture shock.

2. Increasingly, I look at other people with an eternal perspective. I find myself longing, praying that they won't miss it—that they won't spend even one more day missing the wonder and adventure of living life with God—that they won't miss their God-ordained destiny.

3. It has made me willing to have God keep me on a "short leash" so I won't stray away from Him and His ways. I don't want to miss it either.

We have an amazing future! A future that began the day we responded to God's invitation to be His beloved. A future that is growing brighter daily as we hold His hand and let Him lead us and teach us what it means to be His beloved. And a future that guarantees unimaginable joy and adventure as we search out eternity with Jesus.

> The path of the righteous is like the first gleam of dawn, shining ever brighter till the full light of day.
> —Proverbs 4:18

Lord, thank You for this life we share!

Looking at him, she was filled once again with wonder. He loved her.

Sensing her look, he squeezed her hand. "Good job, beloved. Well done."

They had traveled some rough roads in recent days. In fact, it had been the most rugged terrain she had yet experienced. But with her hand held tightly in his, she had come through it.

Now they stood in this amazing place, delighting in their shared joy of being together and viewing the scene before them.

Then he began to speak. His words and gestures, as he spoke of his plans for their future, seemed on the one hand like the telling of a fairytale, while on the other, the unveiling of reality. She watched as the dream he had planted in her heart and nurtured over the years took on form and life before her eyes.

As he spoke, the beauty of his dream spread its glory into the eternity unfolding before her. Captivated by the creative power of his words, she watched, spellbound, as revelation took on substance. Her voice rose with those of the multitudes around her, in wave upon wave of loud, unrestrained exclamations of joy and wonder. For this he had made them his own. For this glorious, unending adventure he had drawn, prepared, and transformed them.

Oh, she liked this place where dreams came true, where every face was that of a friend, and where her beloved shone brighter than the sun and filled every place with his presence...

She awoke to the barking of her neighbor's dog. She lay still as she drifted from dream to reality. As reality pressed her to consciousness, she struggled to hang onto the dream, but could not.

Finally fully awake and feeling somehow cheated, she lay staring at the ceiling.

"Lord, what's it really like? Was my dream anything like Your real heaven?"

With a smile as broad and as bright as the sun, He replied, "Beloved, the adventure has just begun. Stay close, and hold on tight."

ENTER IN ...

Now the dwelling of God is with men, and he will live with them. They will be his people, and God himself will be with them and be their God. He will wipe away every tear from their eyes. There will be no more death or mourning or crying or pain, for the old order of things has passed away.

—Revelation 21:3–4

And they will live happily ever after—and that's no fairytale!

Just a Word ...

My soul clings to you; your right hand upholds me.
—Psalm 63:8

THANK YOU FOR letting me share my story with you. I hope you have been encouraged by what you've read.

Wouldn't it be nice if reading a book about soul healing (or *writing* a book about soul healing) was the end of the matter—if the gap between what we know to be true and our actual experience just disappeared? But the reality for me, and most people I talk to, is that we live in the gap. And I know that's okay—in fact, better than okay. I believe it's right where God wants us. It's a dependent place. And if I've learned anything, it's that I will never outgrow my need to cling to Jesus as He leads the way from brokenness to wholeness. Perhaps, after all is said and done, the goal isn't wholeness so much as learning to cling.

Questions for Reflection and Discussion

Chapter 1: The Invitation

1. What are some common hindrances that keep people from responding to God's invitation to come to Him?
2. Have you ever struggled with feelings of unworthiness related to God's invitation? What made you feel unworthy?

Chapter 2: Love Song

1. How would you explain what is happening with the girl and the Song in the story?
2. What has been your experience of God drawing you to Himself?
3. What common experiences in life can hinder a loving trust of God?
4. Can you give an example from your own experience of having given or received unconditional love in a human relationship?

Chapter 3: Belonging

1. Remember a time when you had a strong sense of belonging. What did you feel? How did it affect your attitude towards yourself? Towards others?

2. Now recall a time when you were hurt by a sense of not belonging. What did you feel? How did it affect your attitude towards yourself? Towards others?
3. What would you say to someone who came to you for help with feelings of rejection?

Chapter 4: Learning to Listen

1. Why does God want to communicate with us?
2. Recall a time when you know God guided you clearly or said something to you that you needed to hear. How did He communicate with you? In what other ways has God spoken to you?
3. What could you do to enhance your two-way communication with God?

Chapter 5: Darkness

1. How would you explain the difference between the darkness talked about in Part 1 and Part 2 of this chapter?
2. What experience have you had with emotional darkness? Spiritual darkness?
3. What has God taught you about dealing with darkness when it threatens to overwhelm you?
4. Can you identify any lies you have believed about God, yourself, or others that need the light of truth applied to them? What are they?

Chapter 6: Grace!

1. What is grace?
2. Do you have any "noisy tin cans" of unfinished business in your life? How do you deal with them?
3. Identify at least one area in your life that was once "unfinished business" but has now either dropped away or been recycled into something useful.
4. What is repentance? Why is it important to make a distinction between self-condemnation and repentance?

5. Was there an aspect of God's grace that stood out to you in this chapter? If so, what was it?

Chapter 7: Whom Do You Serve?

1. What would you say to someone who asked you: What does it mean to serve God?
2. What responsibilities, goals, or dreams drive you? Where do you struggle to live these out within God's grace?
3. In what ways do you serve God? How do you balance "doing" and "being"?
4. What to you is worth dying for?

Chapter 8: God of the Here and Now

1. Do you agree with the statement, "God isn't in a hurry"? If so, in light of the serious needs in our world, why isn't He?
2. What do you think it means for a Christian to live in the "now"? Can you think of scriptures that encourage us to live in the "now"?
3. How would you describe the distinction between living *with* Jesus and living *for* Him? Which do you find more difficult? Why?
4. What could you do to live more consciously *with* God in your everyday life?

Chapter 9: Through the Valley

1. Recall a valley experience you have had or are presently going through.
2. What have you learned about God through your experience?
3. What have you learned about yourself?
4. How can we help one another when we are going through valley experiences?

Chapter 10: Battle Worn

1. Could you identify with the weary soldier in the story? Explain.
2. What do you do when you feel "battle worn"?

3. What aspect of warfare are you most vulnerable to: Pressure to follow your own desires apart from God? Pressure to conform to the ways and values of the culture around you? The battle with the devil's attacks? Give an example.
4. What is at stake in the battle? Why are we fighting?
5. How can you better prepare yourself to win the battles you face?

Chapter 11: Restorer of My Soul

1. Where are you on the journey from brokenness to wholeness?
2. What has God used in the healing process in your life?
3. In what ways are you different today because of God's healing work in you?
4. Do you have a "banging door" or an area of brokenness for which you need to ask God to bring more healing and freedom?

Chapter 12: Into His Presence

1. Were you able to enter into this journey to the pool of refreshing? If so, what was your experience?
2. Why does God invite us to come away and be with Him?
3. What helps you to be quiet and attentive to God? If this is new for you, ask Him to show you how to enjoy time in His presence.

Chapter 13: Ever After

1. How does an eternal perspective on this life change the way we live our lives? How does it change the way we view others?
2. Are any ideas presented in this chapter new to you? Explain.
3. How are you responding to Jesus' invitation to you to personally draw near to Him and be His beloved?
4. Do you have unanswered questions about what it means to be God's beloved? If so, here are a few suggestions: (1) Schedule time with someone who has already begun this journey with Jesus to ask your questions. (2) Read more about God's personal invitation to you in the Gospel of John. (3) Begin your own two-way conversations with God, freely asking Him your questions and then listening for His

loving voice. He promises that if we seek Him, we will find Him. I know it won't be long before you hear Him say, "At last you have come, beloved."

PW

Printed in the United States
147968LV00003BA/30/P